Military Geography

Attention Authors

MILITARY GEOGRAPHY

Dr. M.L. Sali

Reader and Head
Department of Defence and Strategic Studies
(Bhonsala Military College-Nashik)

Manas Publications
New Delhi-110002 (INDIA)

MANAS PUBLICATIONS
(Publishers, Distributors, Importers & Exporters)
4402/5-A, Main Ansari Road
(Opp. HDFC Bank)
Darya Ganj, New Delhi-110 002 (INDIA)
Off. © 23260783, 23265523, Res. © 23842660
Fax: 011-23272766
E-mail: manaspublications@vsnl.com
www.manaspublications.in

ISBN 978-81-7049-324-2
Rs. 495/-

Typeset at
Manas Publications

Printed in India at
Jaico Printers, Delhi
and Published by Mrs Suman Lata for
Manas Publications, 4402/5-A, Main Ansari Road
(Opp. HDFC Bank),
Darya Ganj, New Delhi-110 002 (INDIA)

ACKNOWLEDGEMENT

I express my indebtedness to my reverend teachers Dr. A.S. Dalvi, Professor and Head, Department of Defence and Strategic Studies, University of Pune, Pune–7 and Dr. V.Y. Jadhav, Reader and Head, Department of Defence and Strategic Studies, G.T.P. College, Nandurbar (M.S.) for giving me opportunity to learn and develop an everlasting interest in "Geopolitics and Military Geography". I would like to place on record my deep sense of gratitude to numerous scholars, authors whose books and articles were freely consulted by me while preparing this book. The names along with details are duly acknowledged in the Bibliography.

I am profoundly grateful to my parents, my wife Mrs. Madhuri Sali and daughter Miss. Prachitai and other family members for their constant encouragement and open hearted support during this arduous work. I am extremely thankful to Dr. Vijay S. Khare (Reader), Department of Defence and Strategic Studies, University of Pune, Pune–7, for providing required literature and information to complete this work. I am grateful to Hon'ble Professor and my teacher Major Gautam Sen, former Head of Defence and Strategic Studies Deptt. and B.C.U.D., Director, University of Pune, Pune–7. And, also Major P.B. Kulkarni (Retd.), former General Secretary, C.H.M.E. Society, Nashik–5 who has been a source of inspiration for me to take up such work.

I would like to offer a token of appreciation to all my friends and colleagues especially, Late Dr. D. A. Mandhare, former BOS Chairman, Defence Studies, University of Pune, Pune–7, and also Dr. P. R. Patil (Bapu), BOS Chairman, Defence and Strategic Studies, University of Pune, Pune–7.

I extend my thanks to Lt. S.D. Kulkarni, Dr. P.A. Ghosh, Dr. J.A. Khan, Dr. U.Y. Kulkarni, Dr. V.V. Raje, Dr. Ashwin Bharadwaj, Mr. Rajendra Nawale-Patil, Capt. V.J. Kawale, Mr. R.I. Raut, Prof. Devendra Vispute and the Hon'ble Principal Dr. Mrs. Suchita Kochargaonkar, Bhonsala Military College, Nasik–5 who have cooperated and extended their good wishes for the completion of this work. I am grateful to Prof. Dilip Kute, Head, Deptt. of English and officiating Principal of K. V. N. Naik College, Nasik for necessary corrections and suggestions on various issues relevant to editing the book. It is Dr. (Mrs.) Geeta Sali and Dr. Chetan Sali who have edited the text from all points of view. I am grateful to both of them for their painstaking job. Lastly I express my sincere thanks to Dr. L. A. Khan for suggestions and corrections of computer assistance. Last but not the least, I am also thankful to Manas Publications, for publishing this work.

Dr. M.L. Sali

PREFACE

In the 20th Century relationship between war and Geography forcefully came up as an academic discipline and synonymously the relationship between Man and Enviornment being twisted on account of industrialisation, urbanisation and deforestation. It highlights the facts that the relationship between "Man and Environment" and "War and Geography" is imperishable. In view of this bitter truth it is vital to have study on this aspect and hence an attempt is being made to work on Geopolitics and Military Geography.

The subject i.e. Geopolitics and Military Geography is yet to proliferate as an academic discipline. In India and specially, University of Pune, Department of Defence and Strategic Studies has introduced "Geopolitics and Military Geography" as a paper in the syllabi in U.G. and P.G. courses since Eighties. I have been learning this subject since my student life and teaching for the last sixteen years, at U.G. and P.G. levels. Obviously, this book is an outcome of teaching "Geopolitics and Military Geography" consecutively. While teaching, I immensly thought that the book on the subject "Geopolitics and Military Geography" should be made available in a simple language for exclusive benefit of the students. The basic aim of this work is to put together the available study material for the students, which will enable to literate the students and proliferate this subject upto a certain extent.

The views expressed and work carried out in this book is academic in nature, while being a learner student of the subject "Geopolitics and Military Geography". I accept the responsibility for any error due to incompetence and inadequacy. It is an attempt to contribute towards the required literature.

FOREWORD

Geopolitics and Military Geography are the core subjects in the context of defence of any nation-state. These two academic facets are important and need to be studied further by academicians, policy-makers and executors in the real life to attain the objective of national power of every nation-state, which is a currency through which a nation maintain its power *status quo* and use it for her own existence. Perhaps, due to applicability of geopolitics and its utility to focus on the goals of a nation-state, a geopolitically advantageous position of a particular nation-state, made other disadvantageous nations to feel jealous about the advantageous positions of that nation-state. By making appropriate use of geopolitical advantages, one can reach at its goal of power status. The history of the world nation-states community is very interesting and exiciting due to the reasons that a small nation can make the best use of its geopolitical position to dominate other big nations. Greeks, Ottoman, French, British and German's systematic efforts, with due weightage given to geopolitics and military geography by their strategy-makers and executors, took them to the height of position in comparison with other nation-states. A careful study of geopolitics and military geography contributed to achieve national goal with limited resources by optimising its usage. It also helped them to attain their national goal in a short span of time as well as to remain at the top for a longer period. Such a usage of these co-subjects cannot be neglected for the simple reason that everybody wants to exist with dignity and security.

In the age of advanced science and technology, the world has shrunken with reduction of time taken to commute geographical distances and space, even though geography / space cannot be eliminated. Instead, geographical perception is being considered very crucial in the age of globalisation, to tackle the issues such as locality and globalisation problems of geo-economics, territorial democracy, as well as issues related to security and defence – such as, defending territory by super power(s) or targeting terrorist in the remotest places in the underdeveloped world.

Geographical Information System (GIS) and Geographical Positioning System (GPS) have become more crucial and essential to deal any matter, which has physical existence and vocational value. Geopolitics is the science of the earth, which studies geographical factors, make use of its advantages and disadvantages to attain political objectives in the premises of dynamic world system. Efforts have been made by Mackinder H.J., A. T. Mahan, Houshafer, Spykman, and Clausewits to utilise the advantages and disadvantages of geography with a view to gain advantage for their country. Their basic ideas have become the doctrines of national policies for their countries; or these ideas have become impetus to others to follow certain principles and adopt certain military doctrines and foreign policies. It is for this reason the subject matters of geopolitics and military geography are important to both academicians and practitioners. The students of defence and strategic studies would be benefited by the book, as it is specifically written for them. However, social scientists, students of international relations, security studies and policy-makers may find this book very useful to gain clarity in their perceptions and to understand the factors, which matter in policy-making and policy execution.

I am indeed happy to write this foreword for Dr. M.L. Sali's book.

Prof. Arun Dalvi [Head]
Department of Defence & Strategic Studies
University of Pune

CONTENTS

LIST OF SKETCHES

"The difficulty of any planning in war
is to arrive at
a true picture of the situation, that is strengths
and dispositions
of the enemy, his intentions,
the weather and many factors which
are almost impossible to forecast.
Given all these,
almost anyone could make a good plan;
without them there must be a considerable amount
of guesswork
and risk in planning."

Field Marshal Lord Wavell

1

A STUDY OF GEOPOLITICS

1. INTRODUCTION

The term Geopolitics is new but well-known to Europe due to the "Origin Land" of this discipline. It is the study of Geography & Political Science in relation to the growth of a state. It is one of the branches of earth sciences and a bridge between natural science and political science. Actually the term Geopolitics is the offshoot of geography and political science which proliferated during Pre and Post era of World Wars I and II. Geopolitics is related to the utilisation of geography in the service of National Government. There is no universally accepted definition of Geopolitics. It can simply be defined as follows:

"It's a genuine science which covers the spheres of geography, Political science and economics in relation to the growth of a state. This Geopolitics was originated in the 20th century."[1]

Geopolitics is the study of outstanding features of the situation and resources of a country with a view to determine its status in world politics. **Karl Haushofer,** a well-known Geopolitician explained, "Geopolitics is the science of the earth in relation to the political developments." It's the study of "space" from the view point of "State". Geopolitics implies a systematic and detailed knowledge of the earth, prepared for its use by Government.[2]

1.1 Meaning and Concept

Geopolitics is basically a study of Geographical factors in relation to national and international affairs. Geography involves in every aspect of power politics and international affairs, for example, the U.S.A. v/s Vietnam conflict during the cold war period, the Suez Canal crisis of 1956 or the USSR intervention in Afghanistan in 1979. Geopolitics provides a frame of reference in which an agreement or decision is to be made. Studying Geopolitics means studying the political organisation/state and policies of the state in relations to their geographical environment. The term "Geopolitics" is a broad term, which also deals with the natural resources in relation to the economic development of the country. This discipline focused on the structure of the earth and highlighted on "inequalities" being done by the nature on the earth, for example, resources, fertility of soil, rainfall. On the earth, about 70% of oil deposits are found in the Middle East, West Asia, Persian Gulf.... etc.[3]

Geopolitics studies physical geography i.e. distribution of natural resources, size, shape, location amongst various states. This fact gets confirmed when we analyse the above fact of 200 large and small Nation States' members of the UN. It is apparent that there are great inequalities amongst these States. Some of the large states are very fortunate that they have rich natural resources. For example, China and India, possessing vast natural resources, are on the path of development and becoming a super power. These inequalities have influenced the relations between one state and another or groups of states.

Geopolitics highlights how these "inequalities" have influenced the relationship within international society. It is a pragmatic study which conveys that "isolation" is impossible in international relations. P.R.C.—Peoples Republic of China—came on the path of development only when she came out from the "isolation". "Inequalities" has brought the closer relationship within international society despite certain inequalities. The inequalities have forced us to be "interdependent" whatever the status a country may have, either it is a super power, a developed country, an under-developed country or a less developed country.

In Geopolitics "it is apparent that there are two factors around which Geopolitics is involved in every respect i.e. dynamic as well as static.

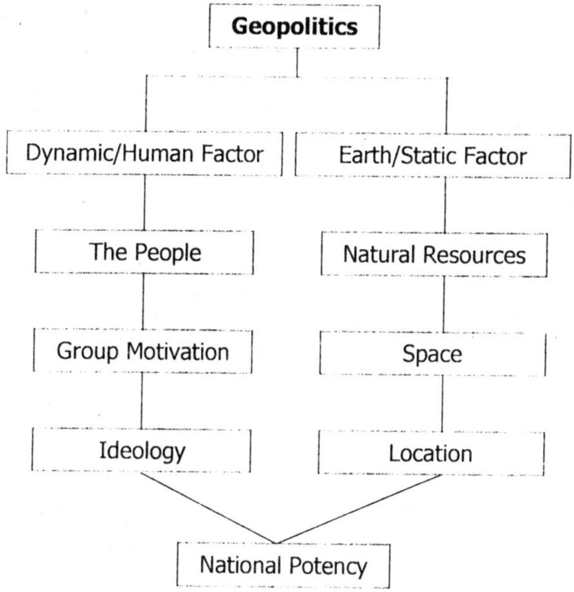

1.2 Field of Geopolitics

Basically, Geopolitics covers an area of Geography, Political Science and Economics and their relevance to the growth of a state. The field of Geopolitics covers the following pre-requisite factors of a state:

1. Territory
2. Population
3. Organising Capacity/Skill
4. Power

1.2.1 Territory

Territory is one of the basic components of a state without which state cannot exist. Every state must have control over the chunk of the earth surface. Territory should be well defined and no discrepancies or ambiguity so far as boundaries are concerned should be left. Within the territory natural and mine resources should be available.[4] It is the prime responsibility of a state to protect her territory and exercise her sovereign power. In the political tenure the Statesman must be able to maintain territorial unity and integrity in a practical manner.

1.2.2 Population

There are advantages and disadvantages of a large population. By virtue of leadership, persuasion, will-power of the peoples and Government, large population can be controlled and mobilised as a "well disciplined force". Over- population creates the pressure on the land and resources which consequently leads to a number of relevant problems—such as lack of food, shelter, employment, crunch of resources, lower standard of living and poverty. All these problems are faced by the Asian and African countries.

The other aspect of population is that some of the states having "poor (less) population" are on the path of development. In such a case land and resources are more than enough for the population which helps them to become a developed country—Sweden, Norway, Denmark etc. In another case, Europe, once upon a time, had a number of problems due to large population but it has got rid of those problems, owing to literacy, hardwork, research and innovation with the help of advanced science and technology. To prevent diversities within the nation-state the equilibrium should be maintained between the existing resources and population.

1.2.3 Organising Skill (Capacity)

Organising a state depend on its historical background and socio-cultural traits. And it varies from one country to another. It is very difficult to predict that one ideology or system is the best and feasible to organise the state in a perfect manner. An idea of sharing power and participation in the decision making process came up as a culmination of the American War of Independence in the 17th century and the French Revolution in A.D. 1789. The 20th century had witnessed that states were organised entirely on the basis of economic equality and justice. This ideology of organising a state on the basis of religion, equal share in power and economic justice introduced a new trend of a conflict i.e. cold war, after World War II. Every system or ideology has merits and demerits, therefore, it cannot be claimed that one is better than the other. Basically it all depends on the leadership, available resources and the will of the mass of population etc.

1.2.4. Power

"Power" means capacity or potency used to achieve the intended goal. Quency Wright defines that "power means a capacity to influence the behaviours of others". But in the present context the word "power" has a wider meaning i.e. political, economic and military.

The political power of a state should be capable of maintaining the law and order effectively and at the same time conducting the foreign affairs in view of protecting national interest. Political power should have control over bureaucrats in order to provide smooth administration to the people. The economic power lies in the production in both the sectors–agriculture and industry. While conducting foreign trade and commerce with international community, attempts should be made to export maximum and import minimum. It is also expected that whatever natural resources and raw materials a country possesses should be exploited fully with foresight and economy. The status of a country within an international community is determined by its "Economic Power" and not necessarily "Military Power", otherwise U.S.S.R. would not have disintegrated. In modern context, "Power means composition of eco-politico-military power.[5]

FUNCTIONS OF POWER

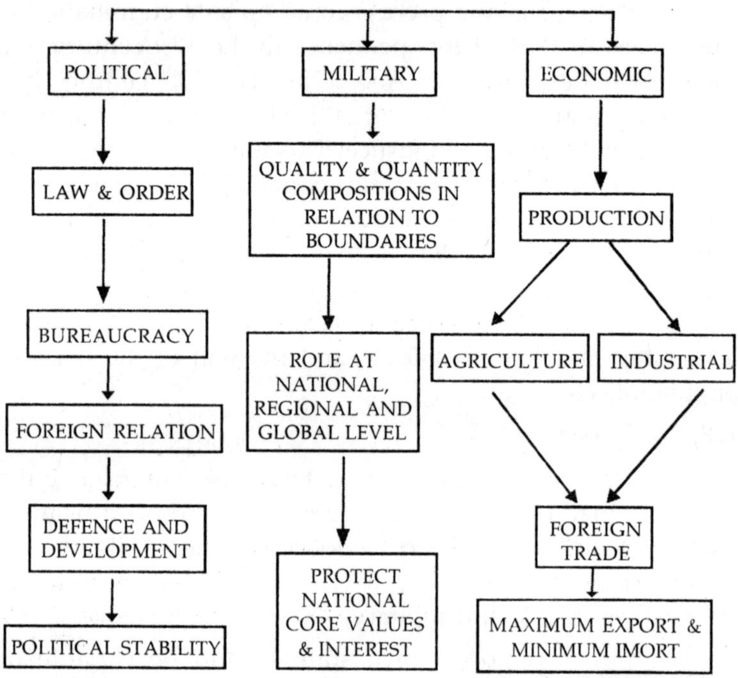

The last component of power i.e. military power which reflects the potential of the country. Existing boundaries should be analysed and accordingly, proportions has to be maintained between the boundaries and strength of the armed forces. Armed forces should be capable to perform their responsibility at internal, external, regional and global levels. The effective role of the armed forces can enhance the status of a country.

In view of the linkages between geopolitics and military affairs, it can be said that geopolitics was devised as an adjunct to warfare. It extended the horizon of Military procedure by two means:

1. *By adding political strategy to the military strategy.*
2. *By pre-conditioning the fighting man for each separate natural environment likely to become a theatre of war.*

1.3. Evaluation of Geopolitical Thoughts

1.3.1 Beginning of the Era of Geopolitics

The 20th century witnessed the "Revolution and Evolution in the field of war, geography, strategy, tactics and weapon system". This 20th century left the milestone for a number of reasons and specially emergence of various geopolitical school of thoughts and its impact on pre-and post-World Wars I and II era. Basically the theory of land, air, and sea powers propounded by geopoliticians has relevance to the state, its growth and power politics. The study of geopolitics would not be completed unless the views and thoughts of contemporary geopoliticians are taken into consideration. Some of the geopoliticians occupied significant place owing to their contribution for contemporary studies of geopolitics. It was the geopolitical thoughts and theories around which state politics at regional and global level moved.

The fact cannot be denied that no geopolitical aspect has been wholly accepted by the world or contemporary society, without certain modifications. The major contribution of geopoliticians is that they had studied systematically on earth factor and acquired its knowledge. Such acquired knowledge about the earth was submitted by them to the societies or their respective Governments for further consideration and use according to circumstances.

1.3.2. An Idea of State

'State' basically, its geographic feature has political identity and it can be indicated on the political map. All the studies of political science and geography alongwith their sister branches have concentrated on state. There were numbers of components of state without which state cannot form and even exist. They are permanent population, definite territory and effective government. In other words no state can exist without territory and no territory can be formed as a state without people. In the light of the above fact, Freidrich Ratsel has a clear idea about state. According to him every state is a part of humanity and one part of land i.e. section of land and humanity is organised as a single unit. The well- known scholar—Pounds—explains that state means "a portion of the earth surface which is organised politically by resident population with effective control and government". It means the monopoly would be enjoyed by government within a specific territory. In modern sense "state" is to be considered a secular and independent institution which acknowledges no authority higher than itself in its own sphere. [6] But owing to globalisation and increasing influence of U.S.A., if the state actors are wrong then freedom, sovereignty or independence of state may be challenged.

1.3.3. Freidrich Ratzel

A well-known German geopolitician had defined the "state as an organism attached to the land". He had been impressed by the ideas of Darwin which reflects in his work entitled "Laws of Spatial Growth of States". He, while comparing a state with organism like species or organism, emphasised that state must have a room to grow for survival. Ratzel suggested certain laws for the growth of a state as follows :

1. The newly conquered territory has to be amalgamated politically to hold it. New territory requires energy and it is the culture which holds the people in a single cultural identity. For example, Indian, Latin, American and African cultures hold the people together.
2. The growth of a state means the faster growth of people—like businessmen, travellers passing, travelling through similar path-routes bringing the people together and close to each other. Such interaction helps the unification of states.
3. The growth of the state also takes place through amalgamation and absorption of smaller states—like Tibet by China in the 1950s.

4. Boundary is the peripheral organ of the state which reflects the strength of the state: So "the growth" of state vows not to attend to the expansion of frontier state but it involves eco-politics, culture etc.
5. For the growth of a state, the statesman must seek rich, fertile and strategically important territory. France had the quest to enjoy the Rhineland territory of Germany in interwar period.
6. Growth of a state has to be stimulated from outside. As such the growth of a state had never advanced without foreign influence. India's nuclear and missile programme would be pointed out as an example in this regard.
7. The growth of a state also depends on the tendencies of statesmen/state actors, towards the "issues" and specially territorial annexation and amalgamation. Hitler of Germany or Mussolini of Italy had aggressive approach towards every affairs of the state. So it depends on the psychology of the leader or state-actor who is in power. Over and above, it is apparent that Ratzel had been attracted by the ideas which had relevance to life sciences. The idea of Ratzel seems to be against peaceful co-existence, sovereignty, freedom and independence of smaller and weaker states. It has lack of objectivity and love for abstractions. However, his theory of the state as a living organism is considered a contribution towards the discipline i.e. geopolitics.[7]

1.3.4 Rudolf Kjellen

He was a Swedish political scientist and professor in Goteborg University and was impressed by geopolitical thoughts of Ratzel. He had agreed that ultimate object of the state was to attend the power. But differing with Ratzel's idea he said, "State need not follow an organic law, i.e. territorial expansion for the "growth of a state". The modern culture and advanced techniques also could solve the purpose of a state and hence no need for "territorial expansion". He had emphasised that states do not need to stress or get involved in struggle for "supremacy" but must acquire natural frontiers externally while in harmony internally.[8] However, he had considered frontier as a shifting zone of assimilation too.

According to him the growth of a state means the territories being transformed from simple geographical areas into cultural-political regions with solidarity, continuity, loyalty and nationality. Kjellen died in 1922 but his ideas have re-emerged as a New Discipline in Germany and were popular as a "German Geopolitics".

1.3.5 Karl Haushofer

Basically he was an officer i.e. Major General in the German Army. In 1919 he had retired from the army and determined to have the re-generations of the German state with the help of geography. He had carried an idea of Kjellen alongwith extension and additions and he called it "Geopolitics". The geopolitics of Haushofer had encompassed the facts of the earth, policies of Government and historical facts of Germany.

Haushofer was appointed as a professor to teach political geography and military science in the institute of "Geopolitics" at Munich in 1924. From 1924 he had devoted himself to educate the German masses along with political elite, regarding "War Geography". He had not only educated the Germans but also proliferated this new discipline called "Geopolitick" throughout the country. There was no single common place throughout the country where Geopolitick was left to be discussed. Geopolitick became a matter of discussion with keen interest at the places like factories, schools, clubs, bookstores, beer-halls and even dinner tables. Haushofer successfully moulded the public opinion in postwar period and generated "consciousness" about Geopolitick throughout Germany. As a result, these institutions became the instrument of national policy and tool of the state and received funds, subsidy and patronage from the Government.

The major contribution of Haushofer was that he had coordinated, integrated and rationalised the whole field of comparative geography. During his stay in Japan he had understood the significance of "space" in power structure and ultimately he propounded the theory of "Living Space", i.e. *Lebensraum*. According to him, the first and indispensable attribute of a state is "living space" which is vital for growth. He had given coherence and direction by the assumption that the German state which was the subject of consecutive growth, must continue her expansion. Basically, the German leaders were ambitious and wanted the revival of the country's previous glory and power. The ideas of Haushofer became an objective of foreign policy of the Nazist in which *Lebensraum* was reflected.[9] But the conquest of Russia by Germany during the World War II was not subscribed by Haushofer.

1.3.6. A.T. Mahan

Alfred Thayer Mahan (1840–1914) was not basically a geographer or a geopolitician. He was a Naval officer in the U.S. Navy. During his service he had successfully shouldered various responsibilities. Even after retirement from services he had continued to work on "Sea Power". By virtue of continuous study and experience he wrote a number of books on sea power and ultimately became a proponent of sea power. He had participated in and guided for long term revolution in the American naval policy.

The essence or summary of his doctrine is as follows:

1. Concentration of Force: If you wish to have control over the sea, the concentration of power is required.
2. War Strategy: It should be formulated only during peace that is during peace be prepared for war.
3. Defensive war: War in terms of morality in character should be defensive but it must be waged aggressive.
4. Control over seas: If you control the sea lanes, then only you would be able to control the whole world.
5. Security of Maritime Boundaries: Without safety and security of maritime boundaries, the protection of land boundaries is difficult. Therefore, maritime boundaries should be the subject of priority.

6. Sea Potential: Sea power should be strong and must be capable of control over the seas and high seas. Credibility and capability is more important to prove our supremacy.
7. Economic Development: Control over the seas and high seas indirectly helps to boost the economic development of the country, as exploitation of resources in territorial water and exclusive economic ones. This will be a contributory factor for national growth, prosperity and security.[10]

A.T. Mahan had an analytical approach and had visualised the significance of "location" of U.K. i.e. Great Britain and concluded that by virtue of insularity, she was secured from external attack. His judgement seems to have proved true and hence U.K. was replaced by U.S.A. as a leading sea power after World War II.

1.3.6 Determinants of Sea Power

Sea Power: The weapons, installations and geographical circumstances enable a nation to control transport over the high seas during war and deny the advantages to the enemy. It is an act of controlling the world sea lanes through the employment of combat ship.

A.T. Mahan established the relationship between the process of development of the country and naval potential. The naval preparedness is vital for overall development of the country. According to him the following factors are most important to determine the status, credibility and capability of the sea power. He had termed them as determinants of sea power.

1. **Location of the State:** The geographical location of the state will decide the nature of boundaries whether it is an Island or connected with lands. The location would be better if it has strategic control of important sea lanes, routes, or bases from which intimation about enemy's arrival could be passed. And it must be easy for communication.

2. **Nature of Coastline:** The nature of coastline will be beneficial if it has natural harbours, estuaries, inlets and outlets. Basically numerous and deep harbours are considered a source of strength and wealth. These should also have depth.
3. **Extent of Territory:** How many kilometers of coastline we have? And either this coastline has certain expected features to defend against enemy or invader. So accordingly, the nature of territory is expected—i.e. feasibility—in every respect.
4. **Size of Population:** Size of population was regarded as an important factor to determine the quality and quantity of Navy. Large populations are considered as source of power. If the country has large population, it can be employed for ship industries, protection of naval bases and even the hold over the colonies and its administrations.
5. **National Character:** It means the people's aptitude for seafaring and commerce, the overall interest of the people for commercial transaction with the outside world. Mahan emphasized "peaceful sea trade" which is vital for the development of sea power.
6. **Policy of the Government:** It will determine whether the best of natural advantages and the richest human resources will materialise to raise the potentiality of the navy. Basically, it means the attitude of the Government towards the development of sea power i.e. bold decisions, policy and incentives by the Government.

According to Mahan the efficient intelligence, strong determination of the Government and desire of the peoples for maritime trade, are the decisive factors for overall development of sea power. [11] The technological and nuclear development has introduced revolutionary changes in warfare; and sea warfare is not an exception. Over and above, naval preparedness is vital for maritime as well as national security.

1.3.7 Prof Mackinder H.J.

Prof Halford John Mackinder was one of the eminent personalities in this new field of "Geopolitics". He was a British geographer who had submitted his research work to the Royal Geographical Society of London in 1904. From 1904 he had modified his work twice i.e. in A.D. 1919 and 1943. He, being a geographer, had noted that three-quarters of the area of the world is water and one quarter is land. By virtue of uniqueness of several oceans and the unity of land masses he had termed as "world ocean" and "world Island" respectively. So within this World Island the Heartland is situated. This Heartland is divided into three areas: **(please see sketch no.1) :**

(a) Pivot Area: The three sides of this area are covered with mountains and the fourth one by the ice bound Arctic. It comprised the Volga river in the west to eastern Siberia in the east and from the Himalayas relevant mountains in the south to the Arctic in the north. Approximately, it covers an area of 9 million sq.miles.

Inner Crescent: This part covers an arch of coastland of Eurasia from Scandinavia to Manchuria. Further, it consists of Europe (except Russia), Middle East, Southeast Asia etc.

Outer Crescent: North and South America, Australia and South Africa in addition to the coastland states or offshores Islands i.e. Britain and Japan.

The essence of his theory highlights the significance of Heartland:

> **"Who rules East Europe (the gateway of the heartland) commands the Heartland, who rules the Heartland commands the World Islands, who rules the World Islands commands the world."**

Prof Mackinder compares this heartland with fortress and focused on its vulnerability in terms of resource potential. This Heartland is bound to emerge as a great colossus in world politics. So whatever may be the critic's opinion about Mackinder's theory of Heartland, the fact cannot be denied that Mackinder was a source of inspiration

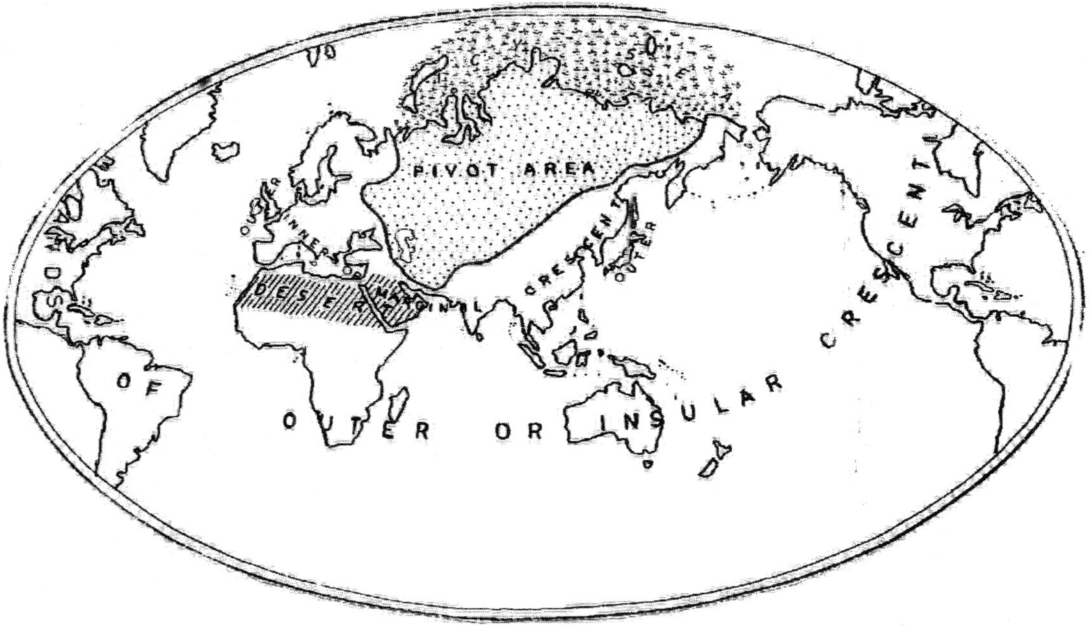

Sketch No.1: **Mackinder's Heartland**

Source: Dr. Shekhar Adhikari "Modern Strategic Thought: Machiavelli To Nuclear Warfare", Kilaso Books, New Delhi,2004

MAP NOT TO SCALE

to geopoliticians. Karl Haushofer had taken the ideas of Prof. Mackinder, i.e. struggle of land-locked versus oceanic peoples and agreed that land power is superior to sea power.[12]

Prof Mackinder analysed the geopolitical position, prospects and the ways how it can control the world. In the cold war period the policy of containment and deterrence is applicable to geopolitical model of Mackinder. Certain demerits and required modifications in this theory of heartland is denied or neglected. He had emphasised that geography of a state is basic to the power potential of a nation and this is a great contribution to the geopolitical thoughts of contemporary world. Mackinder devoted himself to a broader review of global distributions i.e. land, sea and accessibility to the sea.

Summing Up: Twentieth century was a landmark in the history of warfare. The geopolitics is a new discipline coming up as a junction between war politics and geography. In U.S.A. contemporary President Roosevelt and Admiral A.T. Mahan were the first who visualised the significance of the new emerging discipline and recognised geopolitics as an important factor in state planning and foreign policy. Swedish Professor, Rudolf Kjellen gave a name 'Geopolitics' at a time when this science had covered only territorial aspects of the state. A.T. Mahan of U.S.A, Prof Mackinder from Great Britain, Ratzel and Haushofer of Germany had proposed various theories of "Geopolitics" and contributed to its proliferation. Though "Air Power" was developed, such development has only minimised the significance of fundamental concepts of geopolitics. Despite technological advancement, "Geopolitics" holds its own significance even today.

Footnotes

1. "A New Survey of Universal Knowledge", *Encyclopedia Britannica*, vol-10, INC, William Benton Publisher, Chicago, 1989, p. 182 f.

2. Dixit, R.D. *Political Geography: The Discipline and Its Dimensions.* Tata McGraw-Hill Publishing Company Ltd. New Delhi, (1982), pp. 12-13.
3. Precis on "Geopolitics" Department of Defence and Strategic Studies University of Pune, 1982.
4. Adhikari, Sudeepta, *Political Geography,* Rawat Publications, Jaipur, 2002, p. 43.
5. *Ibid* 48-49.
6. Dwivedi, R.L., *Fundamentals of Political Geography* Chaitanya Publishing House, University Road, Allahabad-2, 1990, pp.40-41.
7. *Ibid.,* pp. 25-26 *see also op. cit.,* R.D. Dixit, pp 8-10.
8. *Op. cit.* , Sudeepta Adhikari, 2002, pp. 37-38 and *see also, op. cit.,* R. D. Dixit 1982, p. 11-12.
9. *Op. cit.* , Dwivedi R.L., pp. 28-29 *see also, Op.cit.,* R.D.Dixit pp. 12-13.
10. Adhikari, Shekhar, *Modern Strategic Thought, Machiavelli to Nuclear Warfare,* Kilaso Books, New Delhi-2, 2004, pp. 79-86.
11. *Op.cit.,* R.D. Dixit, pp. 98-102.
12. Adhikari, Dr. Shekhar Halford John Mackinders, "Theory of Heartland: An Appraisal, *Indian Journal of Strategic Studies,* Vol.XXIII, 2002. Defence Studies Department, University of Allahabad pp. 66-71.

❖ ❖ ❖

2

FRONTIERS AND BOUNDARIES: LAND AND MARITIME

2. INTRODUCTION

The terms--Frontier, Boundaries, Line of Actual Control—appear to be synonymous but every terminology has a different meaning though they are co-related. The most important aspect is the 'Boundary', and its security especially Nation-State became very vocal about their boundaries. The International politics was centered on "boundary issue" during the era of post World War II. The boundary issue within nation-state was being subject of emotional attachment, dignity, sense of patriotism, honour, prestige, responsibilities and even sacrifice. And hence it is apparent that during the era of post World War II the wars in Africa and Asia were fought for the settlement of boundary disputes—by use of force.

2.1 Origin of Boundaries

It was only in the 20th century that border issues had a centric issue at regional politics and in global affairs too. In ancient period the Greeks, Romans, Sindhis, neither demarcated their boundaries on actual ground nor even bothered about it. The nations-states became aware of their boundary lines in the 17th century and practised more, particularly after the French Revolutions. It was the Romans, who had an Empire and demarcated the boundaries of their states. Thus the concept of International boundary line came into existence[1] and occupied a significant place in regional and global affairs during the era of post World War II. And hence, it is highly essential to have a proper understanding of various terminologies of peripheral area.

2.2. Various Terminologies

In view of studying geopolitics and military geography, it is highly essential to have a proper understanding of different terminologies concerned with defence and development of a country i.e. Border, Boundary, Frontier and Line of Actual Control.

2.2.1. Border

The term 'Border' itself indicates a meaning. Border means inner area which adjoins with boundary line. In other words, border means an area which extends inward from the boundary line. The depth of the border area depends upon the nature of the terrain and the policy of the concerned Government. For example, Government of India deliberately, not constructed the roads in some of the McMahon line border area with a view to impede Chinese advance into this territory. The border area is normally dealt with "Military Forces" in order to carry out their responsibilities like patrolling, vigilance, operation against enemy and security of boundary line etc.[2] And hence it is considered a "Sensitive Area" and falls under the purview of the military forces, despite the country having a democratic set-up.

2.2.2 Boundary Line

Boundary Line is a line which separates the two sovereign (political units' organisation) states from each other. It's a line of demarcation of political zones determined by the treaties, agreements and conventions by the concerned statesmen and authorities. Boundary means a vertical plane which cuts through the air space, the soil and subsoil of adjacent states. Boundary reflects the limit, a limit of internal political power and is a more effective barrier to socio-economic and cultural exchanges. It is the boundary which binds an area and its people in a single identity under one sovereign government.

The word "Boundary" is a legal concept which has no ambiguity about its location and clarity. The authenticity of boundary is based on the process of delimitation and demarcation. Before demarcation of the boundary on the ground, it is supposed to be delimited on the basis of geography, population, socio-cultural and economic factors with due consideration from the diplomats of the concerned state. An agreement has to be signed with details in the map and once the copy of agreement is exchanged, then it is supposed to be circulated globally to all institutions. It is to be recognised as an "International Boundary". Therefore, it is said that boundary is a legal line between two political-sovereign units.

2.2.3. Frontier

Once Lord Curzon, the then viceroy of British India said:

> *Frontiers are "indeed a Razor edge on which hang suspended" issues of war and peace of life or death of Nations.*

The statement of Lord Curzon reflects the facts of the 'national life'. Basically, frontier is an ancient phenomenon which has no legal base. The term "Frontier" indicates an area which is in the front. Frontier is a politico-geographical area lying beyond the integrated region of the political units and to which expansion could take place. Prof Pounds also highlights the concept of frontier by explaining it thus:

> *"Its border zone, unclaimed, and unused into which people from each side may at time intrude but over which neither side claims or exercise an exclusive control."*[4]

The above explanation indicates that frontier is not a legal concept and has no authenticity. It can be a source of conflict on account of ownership, exact location and number of ambiguities.

The frontier is not an end but a beginning of the state. Frontier, an area lying in the front, does not mean the line but it designates an area which is ahead of hinter land. Frontier is on the margin of the inhabited world. Frontier is encroached by a state without any serious obstacles. In modern age, due to over-population, and political awareness, politicians opine that losing an inch of territory is not affordable under any circumstances. Ultimately, it led towards non-existence of concept of frontiers in a practical sense. Modern world has no place or existence except Antarctica and oceans.[5]

2.2.4 *Line of Actual Control*

The term "Line of Actual Control" indicates that the dispute is yet to be settled and whatever arrangement made is considered as *ad hoc* only. The phrase "Line of Actual Control" is being practised by the concerned countries as a substitute arrangement for the time being—adjustment. When there were territorial disputes regarding ownership of the region or exact location of the boundary in such cases, for reference the line of actual control becomes a reference point.[6] For example, line of actual control between India and Pakistan in Kashmir sector came into existence as a part of territorial dispute. In some cases boundaries were not demarcated on the actual ground due to difficult nature of terrain; so this difficult nature of terrain creates a number of ambiguities, and such ambiguities can be a source of conflict. Sino-Indian border dispute is a distinguished example in this regard. Sino-Indian boundary had never been demarcated on the actual ground due to difficult nature of the terrain. So this non-demarcated boundary became a matter of dispute and hence both the contending powers have been using the term for their reference as a "Line of Actual Control". It has to be remembered that when the dispute is in a dormant situation, then the line of actual control becomes the point of reference.

2.2.5 *Determinants of The Boundary*

Basically the boundary-marking is the job of surveyors and boundary-making is the responsibility of the statesmen. So ambiguity in location, poor visibility or lack of identification marks are an obstacle towards the development of harmonious relations between these contiguous countries.

Hence, peaceful co-existence, development and security are jeopardised in addition to deterioration in bilateral relationship.[7]

In view of the above difficulties, it would be in the interest of respective Governments that they must follow the procedure of "Delimitation" and "Demarcation", (socio-cultural, eco, religious, geographical factors) while finalising boundary. It is to be considered that territorial allocations are vital before delimitation and demarcation. The process of delimitation and demarcation is supposed to be carried out very carefully in order to prevent further ambiguity, conflicts and complications. Delimitation means an actual delineation of the boundary on the paper. This delineation of the boundary line on the paper mainly consisted on socio-eco, cultural, historical, geographical factors with physical verification on the ground and due consideration of the concerned statesmen. Demarcation of the boundary line on the ground has to be done by fixing the identification of marks like, pillars, vistas, walls, barbed fencing etc. There are numbers of criteria like language, ethnic stock, religion, socio-cultural, eco-political setting, physical-features i.e. Geography etc. on which the determination of the boundary line depends.[8]

Functions of Boundaries

There are two major types of boundaries. The first one is Natural and the other one is Artificial. The natural boundaries are determined and practised by the nation-state due to difficult nature of the terrain. And artificial boundaries were determined by the colonial powers as a part of "power politics" in the past. This colonial boundaries created numbers of queries and conflicts for newly independent countries during post World War II era. But natural boundary is being practised with due respect. Sir Thomas Holdich—renowned scholar of political geography highlights the status of natural boundaries. He is of the opinion that:

> *"...of all these natural features a definite line of watershed carried by a conspicuous mountain range is undoubtedly the most lasting, the most unmistakable and the most efficient as a barrier."*[9]

So it is apparent that natural boundaries (except few cases like India-China boundary) are more peaceful rather than artificial and colonial boundaries.

It may be noted that whatever the types of boundaries are, the functions seem to be the same. The functions of boundaries are as follows:

- Legal
- Defensive
- Economic
- Barrier

2.3.1 Legal Function

To control and exercise the power is an important function of the Government. Boundary is a legal phenomenon and hence it has a right to check the illegal activities and even to take legal action against criminals. Taxes must be imposed upon external goods and commodities in order to earn more and more income for the state and to check the illegal emigration and immigration effectively.

2.3.2 Defensive Function

It is an ancient function of the state boundaries. To protect the property, peoples and wealth of the state, boundary has to play its significant role. It is the boundary that defends the state from natural and unnatural threats. But without barbed fencing, construction of wall pillars or vistas, the boundary cannot perform this basic function of defence. An attempt should be made to strengthen it by various measures.[10]

2.2.3 Barrier Function

Boundary is an effective barrier for socio-cultural illegal exchange. Basically, natural features like mountains with chains of high altitude act as natural barriers between the two countries. For example, the Himalayan ranges had acted as a barrier between India and China for a longer period. Boundary is a barrier against wild animals, illegal traffic and even flood. The Chinese "Great wall" had acted as a barrier for a long period against enemy, invaders, animals etc. Whatever may be the nature of boundary, it acts as an effective barrier.

2.3.4 Economic Function

We consider boundary as the limits of a territory, within certain purview. Government has to protect the economic interest of the state through boundaries. Boundary can function effectively to protect the interest of the state. Government can erect traffic walls against outside competition for its market and thus assist internal industries against illegal trade-commerce to control illegal trade against importing and exporting through boundary area, to restrict entry of goods and commodities from outside, to have control over the minerals and other resources etc.

In a nutshell, the function of boundary can be summarised into few sentences. According to Carison "Geography and World Politics":

"The international boundary is a more effective barrier in halting the movement of people, goods and machines than are the widest oceans, highest mountains, most arid desert."[11]

2.4 Contrasts Between Frontier and Boundary

Frontier	Boundary
1. Frontier is a real and it's an area.	Boundary is linear in character, it's a line .
2. Frontier is historical and an ancient phenomenon like history, it may repeat itself but again like history, it is always unique.	Boundary is a modern concept. It's a non-variable phenomenon, determined by treaty and laws and recognised by International community.
3. Frontier is outward-oriented.	Boundary is inward oriented.
4. Frontier is considered as one of contact.	Whereas boundary is considered a definite line of separation.
5. Frontier is a geographical feature.	Boundary is a political feature.
6. Frontier is an absolutely indefinite land and it's no man's land	Boundary may be natural and even artificial, man-made and demarcated
7. It is very difficult to pinpoint	But it is very easy to pinpoint the

	Frontier	Boundary
	the essential features of the frontier which are universally valid.	essential features of which boundary has been accepted and recognised universally.
8.	Frontier has been a rudimentary socio-political relation.	Whereas, boundary has developed socio-political system more than the frontier area.
9.	Frontier has natural historical and traditional base.	Boundary has legal, official and authentic base.
10.	Frontier is outer-oriented and directed towards the outlying areas which is a source of danger and it's not bounded by the center.	Boundary is inner-oriented and it is created and maintained by the will and control of government. It has no life of its own and is coordinated by empirical forces.
11.	Frontier is a manifestation of centrifugal forces.	Whereas boundary is a centripetal force along with range and vigour.
12.	Frontier is not in existence except Antarctica and Ocean. And it is not being practised.	The boundaries are in existence on land, air and sea and practised vigorously.[13]

In view of the artificial boundaries created by colonial powers a number of war had been fought during the post World War II. In the past, boundaries of Afro-Asian countries were demarcated by the colonial powers on the basis of contemporary politically vested interest with several discrepancies. For example, McMahon line between India and China was determined by the Britishers in 1914 during Shimla conference on paper only. This McMahon Line has a number of discrepancies and ambiguities and even after 50 years the differences on McMahon line are yet to be patched-up between India and China.[14]

In this modern, competitive and complicated age, the non-disputed boundaries will stimulate the respective governments and diplomats to play the deserving and legitimate role at regional and global level. It means safety, security and development of a country depends upon a peaceful and well demarcated boundaries. It is highly essential to prevent the disputes over boundary; it should be well defined and demarcated on the ground.

2.5 Maritime Boundaries

The concept of maritime boundary is different from land boundaries. Maritime boundary does not mean the sea coast or shoreline of a concerned state, like land boundaries, it has various terminologies i.e. territorial water, exclusive economic zone, contiguous zone, continental shelf etc. Boundaries on land can be indicated and identified by setting of identification marks i.e. pillars, vistas, barbed fencing; whereas it is difficult in the high seas to point out an end of various limits of maritime boundaries. But it may be marked on charts. It is to be ensured by sailors or navigators that sovereignty of a concerned state should not be violated. The circumstances in ocean are complicated. It is difficult to identify the violation of territorial water or exclusive economic zone. No one can be assured whether the ship is within limit or beyond it. Such uncertainty provokes the conflict within the concerned states. So, in order to prevent such tenseful circumstances and conflict, the international community has formulated certain codes for conduct of freedom, sovereignty by states in high seas.[15] The "code" i.e. the law of sea has been subject to amendments by the international community under the banner of "United Nations Convention on law of the sea", from time to time. In 1982, 159 states signed the convention on the Laws of the Sea.

2.5.1 Territorial Waters

According to convention on the law of the sea, territorial waters mean the belt of sea is adjacent to the coastal state. It is located at some distance from the coast and marks the outer limit of the territorial waters of the states. Every state has the right to establish the breadth of its territorial sea upto a limit not exceeding 12 nautical miles, measured from baselines determined by UN convention on the laws of sea. The state has a right to conduct absolute sovereignty over it—not meant only over the territorial waters but also over air space and over the territorial sea as well as to its bed and subsoil. To defend the territorial waters from hostile activities by the adversaries has been a challenging task. This task becomes more difficult and complicated due to use of bombers, missiles, submarines and efficient radar system. This concept of territorial waters came into existence in the 17th century at the beginning while its limit was only three miles. The United States in 1793 had restricted herself upto three miles as a limit of its territorial waters.

2.5.2 Continental Shelf

Basically, it is a geographical and geological concept. This concept of continental shelf is not new. The coastal state has sovereign right to explore and exploit the marine resources only. It is to be noted that despite their economic significance, the shelves are never claimed by states. Article 78 of the UN convention on the law of the sea highlights the rights of the coastal states over the continental shelf do not affect the legal status of the superjacent waters. It was the United States of America who tried to define the concept of continental shelf. According to U.S. States Department press release of 18th Sept 1945: The continental shelf means "Submarine land which is contiguous to the continent and which is covered by no more that 100 Fathoms (600 fist) of water". In 1958 conference at Geneva, one of the most important aspects of "Continental Shelf" was intensively discussed.[17] The continental shelf can be defined on the basis of convention on the Law of Sea. The continental shelf of a coastal state comprises the sea-bed and subsoil of the submarine areas that extend beyond its territorial sea through the natural prolongation of its land territory to the outer edge of the continental margin, or to a distance of 200 nautical miles from the baselines from which the breadth of the territorial sea is measured where the outer edge of the continental margin does not extend upto that distance.[18]

2.5.3 Contiguous Zone

Contiguous zone means a "zone" which has contiguity with "territorial water (sea)" of the coastal state. The concerned or adjacent state can exercise her control over it.

According to U.N. conventions on the Law of the sea, 1982, article 33 explains the concept and functions of the contiguous zone. Contiguous zone means, in a zone contiguous to its territorial sea, wherein the coastal state may exercise the control necessary to:

1. Prevent infringement of its customs, fiscal immigration or sanitary regulations within its territory or territorial sea.
2. Punish infringement of the above regulations committed within its territory or territorial sea.[19]

Contiguous zone imposes few restrictions on the freedom of the high seas. Thus contiguous zone may not extend beyond 24 nautical miles "baseline" from which the breadth of the territorial sea is measured.

2.5.4 Exclusive Economic Zone

Exclusive economic zone is a terminology of the maritime boundaries. It is an area beyond and adjacent to the territorial waters and the limit of this exclusive economic zone is two hundred nautical miles from the baseline. According to the U.N. convention on law of sea article 56, the coastal states have sovereign rights for the purpose of exploring and exploiting marine resources including seabed and subsoil. State also has a right over artificial islands, marine scientific research as well as protection and preservation of the marine environment within the exclusive economic zone. During UN conference on the law of the sea held in 1977 and 1982–83, certain laws of the sea like inclusion of fisheries and resources of the seabed within EEZ were modified. The UN convention on the law of sea also provides the right of the hot pursuit to the coastal states if their sovereignty is violated.[20] The exclusive economic zone has a determinant role in the process of development of the country subject to proper exploration and exploitation of the exclusive economic zone.

Footnotes

1. Martin, Ira and Hami, Blij, *Systematic Political Geography*, John Willey and Sons, New York, Chinchester, Toronto II, editor, 1973, pp. 136-138.
2. Sharma, R.C. and Arya, D.K. Editor, *Management Issues and Operational Planning for Indian Borders*, Scholar Publishing Forum, New Delhi, 1991, p.13.
3. Pounds, Norman J.G., *Political Geography*, McGraw Hill Book Company Inc, 1963, pp. 57-59.
4. Ladis K.D. Kristof, *The Nature of Frontiers and Boundaries*, Seminar Paper, University of Chicago.
5. Sali, Dr. M.L. *India China Border Dispute*, Ashish Publishing Corporation New Delhi, 1998, pp. 18-19.
6. Martin, Ira and Hami, Blij, III Edition, *op. cit.*, 1980, p.84.
7. Sharma, R. C. and Arya, D. K. Editor *op. cit.*, p.13.
8. Murthy, T.S. *Path of Peace;- Studies on Sino-Indian Border Dispute*, ABC Publishing House, New Delhi, 1983 pp. 38-42.
9. Choudhary, A.P. *Military Geography*, Nirali Prakashan, Pune, 1995, Marathi edition, p. 189.
10. Dwivedi, R.L. *Fundamental of Political Geography*, Chaitanya Publishing House, University Road, Allahabad, 1990, pp. 141-143.
11. Chaudhary, A.P. *op. cit.*, p.193.
12. Adhikari, Sudeepta *Political Geography*, Rawat Publication, New Delhi, 2002 pp. 223-224.
13. Dixit, R. D. *Political Geography: The Discipline and Its Dimensions*, Tata McGraw Hill Publishing Company, New Delhi, 1982., pp. 59-60.
14. Sali, Dr. M.L. *op. cit.*, p. 244.
15. Sukhwal, B. L. *A Political Geography*, Allied Publishers, Mumbai, 1971 p. 34.
16. Kapoor, Dr. S. K. *International Law*, Central Law Agency, 30D/1, Motilal Nehru Road, Allahabad 1994, p. 303.
17. Adhikari, Sudeepta 2002, *op. cit.*, p.239
18. Kapoor, Dr. S.K. *op. cit.*, p.311
19. Dwivedi, R.L. *op. cit.*, p.167 (see *also* Dr. S.K. Kapoor, *op.cit.*, p.307)
20. Kapoor, Dr.S.K. *op. cit.*, 324.

❖ ❖ ❖

3

BUFFER AND LAND LOCKED STATES

3. INTRODUCTION

The term "Land Locked" and "Buffer States" are different from each other. The term "Buffer" indicates that it is a "Man Made" concept and had been used as means or technique of power politics. And "Land Locked" state means the country which has no sea and this particular chunk of territory (State) is deprived of sea coast. It is very essential to study both the terminologies, without which the study of Geopolitics, Military Geography, and International Relations would remain incomplete.

3.1 Meaning and Concept of Buffer States

Buffer and Land Locked states are the subject of "Geopolitics" and political science. Basically a Buffer State is the political phenomenon and Land Locked state is a natural one. Except this basic difference there are various similarities regarding the problems and prospects of the land locked and buffer states. It is highly essential to study the problems and prospects of land locked and buffer states. Buffer state means a state which is located between two great powers or possibly belligerents. A buffer state lying between two rival or hostile states by virtue of its sheer existence is thought to prevent conflict between them. The invasion of a buffer state by any one of the powers surrounding, will often result in war between the powers.

The creation of buffer state had been adopted as one of the techniques for maintenance of "Balance of Power". It is assumed that buffer state is a weak state and located between two powerful states. In the past buffer states were purely considered as a mechanical device of international politics.

Buffer state separates physically two potential warriors making it more difficult for them to exchange "blows". Buffer states have to adjust the tension of the two political voltages.[1]

Historical Record: In the past Afghanistan for longer period acted as a buffer state between Imperial Russia and British India. 'Tibet' also had played a role of buffer state between Imperial China and British India, Mongolia was the buffer state between the Peoples Republic of China and the Soviet Union (now Russia). Poland also acted as buffer state between Germany and the Soviet Union. In order to minimise the potential of the hostile states during 20th century, an attempt had been made to create the buffer state.[2] During interwar period, France had motivated the peoples of Rhineland to continue their struggle for "Independent State" from Germany. If the peoples of Rhineland would had attained independence from Germany, the Buffer State i.e. Rhineland could have come into existence.[3] In the eighties Pakistan also had motivated the peoples of Punjab state of India to have an Independent state of Khalistan from the Government of India. The Pakistani design to create a "Khalistan" as a buffer state between India and Pakistan and minimise the threat to their triangular heartland, had been brushed aside by "Operation Blue Star and policies of Indian Government".[4]

Buffer states are of great importance due to their cushioning effect between great powers. They may be neutral or neutralised states, satellite states or dependent territories and even there may be more aggregations of power in a relative honourable role. This is an area of weak state's vast distance, for geographic barrier and endless conflicting interest of the great powers as well as geopoliticians.

3.2 Meaning and Concept of Land Locked State

Land locked state means a state which has no sea coast at all and has only land boundaries and is not at all directly connected to the ocean. It is "nature" that deprived such a state from sea coast—ultimately water resources and maritime trade and commerce. A country completely surrounded by land boundaries is quite opposite to an Island.

Some of the countries, despite having coastline are treated as a land locked seas such as the Caspian Sea and the Aral Sea. These seas are considered to be lakes and since they do not allow access to seaborne trade countries such as "Kazakhistan" are still considered to be land locked. Once upon a time being "land locked" was regarded as a disadvantageous position. But by virtue of advancement in science and technology, interstate dependency and the concept of Global village "land locked states" can also survive.[5] There are 42 land locked states in the world.

Problems of Land Locked/ Buffer States

Land Locked/Buffer States are in a helpless position and the international community is expected to deal with them "sympathetically", the problems of these countries are as follows:

(a) Land locked states are not able to conduct maritime trade and commerce independently. They are dependent on their 'neighbours'.

(b) They have to spend maximum amount for "transportation" in order to have an access to "sea coast" from their base. In view of this practical difficulty, very poor amount remains to be concentrated on development and other activities.

(c) Security of these states can be questioned by neighbours. Freedom, sovereignty and independence may be violated by potential neighbours. As China had bulldosed Tibet and her freedom, sovereignty were sealed forever in 1951.[6]

(*d*) It is very difficult for these countries to formulate the foreign and defence policies, independently without any pressure. Defence policy or to take independent decision on any global issue seems to be difficult for these countries.

(*e*) If the neighbours have different types of ideology, then it becomes a great headache for these countries to make both the countries happy at a time. It requires a great diplomatic skill. Like Nepal, Bhutan, their "Rulers" are trying to satisfy Democratic India and Communist China at the same time.

(*f*) During war or conflicting situation, it's very difficult to maintain the "neutrality" and keep aloof from actual conflict.

(*g*) History of has warfare has witnessed that these States were the subject of interference and intervention from time to time by the great powers. History of Afghanistan and Balkan states support this fact.[7]

3.4 Prospects (Solutions)

Taking into consideration the problems and practical difficulties of buffer and land locked states, the international society i.e. Nation State and specially the relevant neighbours must deal with them on "humanitarian ground".

The nation state or concerned neighbours should not take the due advantage of their helpless position.

1. All Buffer/Land locked states should not be the subject of exploitation by neighbours or super powers.
2. 'Freedom', 'sovereignty' and 'independence' of such states must be respected by neighbours.
3. In addition to the "International Law", on the basis of humanity and morality the neighbours of a land locked states, should offer the maximum facilities for accession of sea coastline, port etc.

4. As far as economic collaboration, assistance or transfer of technology are concerned the neighbour or supplier should not impose difficult terms and conditions on land locked or buffer state.
5. World Bank, UN, Super Powers and developed countries must provide maximum financial aid and loan at minimum rate of interest. Attempt should be made to provide maximum developmental facilities and opportunities for the development of these countries.
6. If the river is flowing between the two countries, the land locked/buffer state should be permitted for maximum use of the "River".
7. World Government i.e. UN and even Super Powers should assure the "security" of Land locked and Buffer states.

Existing Facilities and Historical Example

According to "United Nations Convention on the Law of the Sea", Land locked states have a right to access to and from the sea without taxation of traffic through transit states. The United Nations have an action plan to assist such land locked states. In the world there are two countries to be treated "Doubly land locked", a person from these countries i.e. Liechtenstein in Europe and Uzbekistan in Central Asia has to cross at least two borders to reach a coastline. Their land locked neighbours do have indirect access to sea via the Danube river in Liechtenstein's case via canals from the land locked but non-freshwater (Caspian Sea) in case of Uzbekistan.

The history of international relation has a record of such cooperations. In post World War I era, Poland was given the Danzig corridor to give it an access with seacoast. The Danube River was internationalised with a view to have secured access to the sea for land locked states of Austria and Hungary.

LAND LOCKED STATES IN THE WORLD

Afghanistan	**Kazakhstan**	**San Marino**
Andorra	Kosovo	Slovakia
Armenia	Laos	South Ossetia
Austria	Lesotho	Switzerland
Azerbaijan	Liechtenstein	Tajikistan
Belarus	Luxembourg	Tibet
Bhutan	Malawi	Transistria
Bolivia	Maldova	Turkmenistan
Botswana	Mali	Uganda
Burkina Faso	Mongolia	Uzbekistan
Central African Republic	Nagorno-Karabakh Republic	Vatican City
Chad	Nepal	Xingjian
Czech Republic	Niger	Zambia
Ethiopia	Paraguay	Zimbabwe
Hungary	Republic of Macedonia/Macedonia	
Inner Mongolia	Rwanda	

Footnotes

1. Norman J. Pounds, *Political Geography*, Mc-Graw Hill Book Company, New York 1972 p.63.
2. Mishra K.P., *Afghanistan In Crises*, Vikas Publication House, Ghaziabad, UP. 1981, p.13.
3. L.N. Srivastava, *International Relations*, Surjeet Book Depot, New Delhi, 1985 p.27
4. *Indian Experts*, Mumbai, 23rd Jan 1991, Editorial Page.
5. Norman J. Pounds, *op. cit.*, p.101.
6. *Ibid.*, p.64.
7. *Ibid.*, p.102
8. http:// www.un.org/special-rep/ohris/11do/default.htm, Land locked Developing Countries.

✣ ✣ ✣

4

AN UNDERSTANDING OF GEOSTRATEGY

4.1 INTRODUCTION

Geostrategy is a new term which focused on the relationship between "war and geographical factors". Basically "Geostrategy", the composition of two different disciplines, has linkage with war and geography. "Geo" is a Greek word, which means the earth i.e. earth presenting factors like land, weather, location – the geography of concerned area. And "strategy" means art of planning for conducting a military operation or war. Geo + strategy mean the study of land i.e. possible battlefield, in relation to the conduct of war. S.T. Das, a well known scholar, defines Geostrategy as—

> *"...the science of geopolitics that deals with strategy; the combination of geography and world problems along with strategic factors characterising a particular geographic region."* [1]

Thus it is clear that "Geostrategy" has linkage with geography, power and strategy. Geostrategy is not an independent discipline but a branch of geopolitics. During the 20th century the "Geostrategy" was the resilient core of the larger subject. Geostrategy treats the warfare as total, encompassing the entire population, resources and scenario of the contesting state.[2] It recognised the psychological effects of the geography of the war theatre on fighting forces. It can be said that Geostrategy was the main theme of the Geopoliticians.

4.2 Factors of Geostrategy

In view of the changing nature of war, Geostrategy does not deal with war and local geography only but also with strategic factors like population and its standard of living, natural resources like life stock; industrial capacity, transportation, net work of the enemy's territory or area of operation. Geostrategy is a phenomenon which deals with geography—power and strategy—at a time in relation to conduct of war. It also assesses the war potential of the country. The factors of Geostrategy are narrated below.

4.2.1 Size and Shape

The size and shape of the country is a subject of stable element of National power i.e. Geography of the Nation. On account of political development or upheavals, the size of the country may be reduced or increased like the disintegration of USSR. There are certain advantages and disadvantages of a larger size country. The large size country provides defence in depth. If the country has got a large size, it possesses a variety of population, climate and resources. But at the same time, there are some disadvantages of a large size. Like defence, preparedness would be very costly—preparation of network for surface transportation, maintenance of communication, then carrying out process of assimilation along with administrations would be difficult. By virtue of variety of population including socio-cultural, language, ethnic difference, the maintenance of National unity, integrity and security would be challenging. Whatever may be the fact, it cannot be denied that "large size" has its own benefits. This may be the reason that China has emerged as one of the super powers.

From the strategic point of view, "shape" has got a determinant role in the process of "development". Shape should be integrated and feasible for internal transportation and communication. The compact shape minimizes the cost of transportation between peripheral and core areas of the power. The shape must be suitable for mobilisation of the armed forces.[3] India's shape has a lot of demerits i.e. Siliguri strip or bottle neck which establishes the link between north-east region and the rest of the country. Either China or Bangladesh or both could close the corridor at will. There is no solution to this visible threat.[4]

4.2.2 Location

"Location" includes latitude and longitude, land and water bodies, in relation to the other States. The country, with its important sea routes and air routes pass has decisive military, political and economic advantages, such location is called a strategic location.[5] Strategically located or important countries like Iran, Pakistan, Egypt, Israel and now Kuwait have become a centre for super power politics. It will not be the Government or people to decide the "nature of defence preparedness" of the country, but it is the location of state that can decide. The maritime location of Belgium and Holland has given them an urge for political expansion backed by naval power. The location of U.K. has an impact on the history of the growth and decay of its political and military leadership in world affairs.

4.2.3 Climate

Climate definitely plays a crucial role in the process of development and security of the country. The efficiency of 'Man and its health' has a great relevance to the climate. It is the climate which is being considered as one of the factors of tactical planning for combat-operation. It is the climate which has long term influence on the physical properties of soil and determines the cropping pattern, dietary habits, physique and attitude. The required rainfall and the agricultural development depend on the "climate".[6]

During hot summer man cannot work hard or even during cold winter, and extreme cold, man will not be energetic. If the rainfall is uncertain and periodically there are droughts, the development of the country is automatically restricted.

It is difficult to claim that certain climate is more suitable, energetic or cheerful or feasible for the development of the country. But generally it has been said that intermediate type of climate is suitable for the development of the country.

4.2.4 Boundaries

Frontier is an ancient phenomenon and finds no place in modern age. It is also not in existence except "Antarctica and Oceans". Boundaries of the states should be natural and must be peaceful. Boundary is artificial, so it should be delimited and demarcated on actual ground. Such non-demarcated boundary becomes a source of conflict amongst the adjoining states due to its economics or strategic importance.

Disputed territories and border area is certainly an obstacle towards the development of harmonious relations between the concerned countries. Hence peaceful coexistence, development and security are jeopardised. The boundaries may be mountains, rivers; bodies of water, but these should act as a barrier effectively and protect the core area i.e. heartland, production centers including components of economic factors of war potential.

4.2.5 Resources and Life Stock

The term "Resources" is considered in a wider context i.e. Natural Resources, Minerals, and (life stock) Raw Material. Natural resources are considered a gift by nature, and raw material can be produced by human efforts, like cultivation of rubber, teakwood or gum etc. As minerals have assumed a prerequisite for Industrialisation, no nation can achieve industrial development without its own adequate stockpile. The natural resources, minerals and raw materials are the pillars of Industrialised Nation; without it a Nation cannot attain the status of "Super Power".

A Nation must have fertile soil, adequate rainfall, flora and capacity to produce foodstuffs. "Food" is essential for every human being and it is in the interest of every country that it should be self-reliant in food production. Dependency on food is considered to be a permanent weakness in international relations. For the procurement of food, clothing, and various requirements of the country, priority should be given to agricultural sector. Forest is one of the major sources of raw material which is vital for industries; without it industrial network cannot function effectively. Ocean is also a source of varied life-stock for which exclusive economic zone and territorial water are exploited, by a number of countries. For industrialisation and defence preparedness steel is most important but unless adequate deposits of iron and metals are there, one cannot carry out the process of development, industrialisation and even defence preparedness of the country.[8]

In view of the increasing population especially in the (Asian and African) third world countries, there is a crunch of resources. For power production it requires the energy resources i.e. coal, oil, natural gas, solar, while energy resources are inadequate. No one is independent in energy resources.

4.2.6 Population (Manpower)

Population is one of the important elements of national power. It has an emotional attachment with the nation. The nation can buy anything from abroad like oil, natural gas, coal, iron, gold, but cannot buy devoted and dedicated "Man Power". Even the Mercenary army can fight the war but you cannot find the sense of patriotism, love and affection for the country.

Population is the basic source of "Man Power". Even a large population can prove a source of power but subject to controlling over the increasing population with discipline. Without control over increasing population and lack of discipline, large population would be a great handicap to the process of 'development'.

In modern age large population is required to fight a war against an enemy for various purposes and fronts—land, air, sea, space, labs, deposits, mines, industries, farms, fields etc. Population is required to fill up the vacuum in the armed forces being created during war. A large population requires holding the territory being conquered from the enemy. Large population is the source of power that may be one of the reasons for the rise of China as a supper power. Large population can be employed for transportation, industries, agriculture and research sector. There are certain demerits of large population as crunch of resources and its relevant problems. The countries have become aware of it. In future strict control over increasing population and growth ratio of infertility may lead the crunch of man power.

4.2.7 Transportation and Communication

Transport is the *de facto* barometer of economic, social and commercial progress and is an indispensable part of culture and the hall mark of civilisation. It is the transport and communication system which enables the region to get rid of natural isolation from the rest of the world.

The network for surface transport should be well developed. Such developed network is helpful for "national integration", people to people contact, exchange, trade commerce. By virtue of such facilities people will come out of their isolation for economic and industrial development, the network of surface transportation is required. The people will be able to break up the regionality—isolation—and become the part of process of assimilation. If the adequate roads, bridges, railway tracks, maritime and air route are available and linkup with the coal-mines, oil deposits, industries, administrative installation, then such network can prove very beneficial for "mobilisation process" and even smooth conduct of war within the country. Therefore, from Heartland to peripheral area the excellent network of transportation and communication is expected. Communication is the key to have the interaction, unity and integrity within the country. During war the network of air, land, and maritime, transportation should be able to reach upto the border or desired place without any difficulty and in no loss of time. Communication (signal) network should be able to "catch-up" the intercommunication of the enemy and at the same time it is to be ensured that enemy would not be able to trap the intercommunication of our combat forces. Strategically, it is in the interest of the country that the routes—air and land and maritime waterway — along with substitute network should be made available.[9]

4.2.8 Industrial Capacity

Industrial capacity is one of the major components of National power. Geostrategically, industrial capacity is also being considered as one of the parameters to decide the status of a country in international community. It is true in the real sense of the term that no "nations" can attend the status of super power without "industrial potential" and this would be decided by the range, variety and nature of production. Industrial potential will be determined by technological know-how, capital investment, skilled manpower and availability of strategic resources and minerals within the country. Industrial capacity is one of the key elements for economic development of the country. An industrial complex should have the much needed capability to produce all the required goods and commodities, war material within the country, without any foreign assistance.[10] In a nutshell, it should be capable to produce goods from pins to tanks. Maximum goods should be exported, after fulfilling the requirements of the existing population within the country. During war the security and safety of industrial complex should be maintained for successful conduct of war. It is to be mentioned that strategic industrial factories are the basic target of the enemy. As a part of economic warfare and hence safety and security are to be maintained accordingly.

4.2.9 Economic Development

Economic Development reflects the overall "image", status and position of the country through the expected GNP, GDP and the ratio of development. A country should attain the overall development in every respect like adequate "network" of air, maritime and surface transportation. The people should be able to avail of basic requirements i.e. food, shelter, clothing, employment with ease. Such development has to be reflected by having maximum foreign currency and good standard of living of the peoples. The overall financial condition of the country should be sound.

No country can conduct the war, for a longer period without the financial base. And in the absence of sound economy a country cannot continue the war. As far as development is concerned, it is expected that overall national life should be healthy, comfortable and satisfactory. Such economic development depends upon the availability of resources within the country—industrial set-up, market, advanced technology, self-sufficiency and will power of the citizens of the respective countries.

4.2.10 National Unity and Integrity

To maintain the national unity and integrity is a challenging task in today's scenario. Without national unity, a country cannot sustain war. The peoples from various communities, languages and regions should support the government during the conduct of war. Justice, balanced developments, and impartial allocation of national resources to the various section of the society would be the best remedy to strengthen the national unity and integrity. If the peoples are integrated and inspired through the process of assimilation, they can work hard in pursuit of aim and objectives of the country despite the diversity in terms of language, religion, and even race.[11] The political parties or religious leaders should not use such a diversity of religion, language, race as an instrument of achieving vested interests. This is to be understood that united and integrated population with a sense of patriotism is one of the source of a national power, especially the population in peripheral area is the most important one from the strategic point of view.[12]

During war the local population of the border area is to play a very crucial role. It has been proved as a fact from time to time. And hence such population should not be neglected by any means. The top priority should be given to the population of peripheral area in the process of assimilation.

4.2.11 Defence Preparedness

It should be based on consideration of geographical facts of the peripheral area. The ratio between space and composition of the armed forces has to be maintained vigorously. It is to be mentioned that armed forces should be well disciplined, trained and equipped with more sophisticated weapons and equipments as compared to those of the enemy. It would be in the interest of the country that defence preparedness needs to be consistent on strategic and tactical aspects. The ally or military alliances had to be organised according to necessity, national interest and international scenario. While purchasing or producing armaments, strategic and tactical analysis has to be made alongwith changing dimensions of threats and security perceptions. Synonymously, the defence planning alongwith foresight and flexibility is to be chalked out.[13] In the process of defence preparedness, developmental activities should not be neglected. Moreover, an attempt for co-relationship is to be established between defence and development. Political elites of the country have to be assured that industrial capacity and economic development would remain as the supporting factor in the process of defence preparedness.

The study of Geostrategy is required:

(a) To determine the aims and objectives of a country.

(b) To enhance the national power.

(c) To chalkout the combat operational planning.

(d) To formulate the foreign and defence policy of the country.

(e) To analyse the Geostrategic position and importance

Footnotes

1. S.T. Das, *Geostrategy*, Kitab Mahal Agencies, Ramdas Peth, Nagpur, Allahabad, 1986, p.1.
2. "A New Survey of Universal Knowledge", *Encyclopedia Britannica*, Vol.No.10, INC, William Benton Publisher, Chicago 1959, p.182H.
3. U.R. Ghai, *International Politics*, New Academic Publishers Co., Jalandhar 1989 p. 134.
4. Balakrishnan Nair, *Facts of Indian Defence*, S. Chand & Co., Ramnagar, New Delhi, 49. 1985, pp. 56-57.
5. R. L. Dwivedi, *Fundamentals of Political Geography*, Chaitanya Publishing House, University Road, Allahabad, 1990, pp. 54-55.
6. U.R. Ghai, *op.cit.*, p.135
7. Ira, Martin and Hami Blij, *Systematic Political Geography*, John Wiley and Sons, New York, 1973, pp.136-138.
8. Majid Husain, Editor, *Resources Geography*, Anmol Publications Pvt. Ltd., New Delhi, 2000, pp. 1-4.
9. S.T. Das, *op.cit.*, pp. 5-7.
10. U.R. Ghai, *op.cit.*, p.142
11. S.T. Das, *op.cit.*, p.13.
12. M.L. Sali, *India China Border Dispute*, APH, New Delhi, 1998, p. 212.
13. S.T. Das, *op.cit.*, pp. 20-21.

✣ ✣ ✣

5

GEOSTRATEGIC POSITION AND IMPORTANCE: COUNTRIES, ISLANDS AND TERRITORIES

5.1 INTRODUCTION

Location is the genuine factor to determine the significance of a concerned state in relation to the external world. Jules Cambon, a French diplomat stated that *"the geographical position of the nation is the cardinal factor conditioning its foreign policy"*. The military evaluation of the location of a state requires a careful assessment. The location of a state affects accessibility, vulnerability, manoeuverability, strategic quality, political sensitivity and national policy. It must be remembered that the military evaluation of political area and geographical location would be "changed" on the basis of technological invention, art, and instrument of war.

Geostrategic location is very significant for its owner and even to the enemy. This "position" provides strategic consideration or benefit to its owner, during war and peace. And this position has a subject of global strategy and directly or indirectly is always in "focus" at national or international level. Tentatively states, regions and Islands of Geostrategic importance may be considered as follows:

- Israel
- Afghanistan
- Kuwait
- Siachen Glacier
- Diego Garcia
- Andaman Nicobar and Lakshadweep
- Antarctica

5.1 Israel

On 14th May 1948 the seeds of one of the international conflicts were sown by the creations of Israel as a state by the Jews. The creation of Israel caused one million Palestinians lost their homes and became refugees in their own land.[1] The birth of Israel has relevance to the issue of Nationalism, Security, Justice, Peace, territory and one of the points for escalation. Palestine (Israel) is bounded on the north by Lebanon, on the east by the Jordan rift and Syria, on the south by the Gulf of Aqaba and on the west by the Sinai Peninsula, Egypt and the Mediterranean Sea.[2] *(sketch no.2)*

From geographical point of view it seems that the boundaries of Israel are artificial. It has physical contiguity with the Arab States. It will be over-simplification to ascribe the conflict in the Middle East solely to the Arab-Jew rivalry. In fact, the very process of establishment of the state of Israel is closely related to the desire of the great powers for domination in these sensitive regions. This territory is the oil wealth of the region which attracts the super powers' attention and intervention.[3] Israel was and is viewed as a "Western Agent" planted in the Middle East to ensure western domination. The war of Arab Israel in 1956 introduced the power vacuum being filled by America on account of withdrawal of the UK and France from this region.[4] It is needless to mention that Israel is a puppet of America to check the Russian influence and now the Chinese influence in this area.

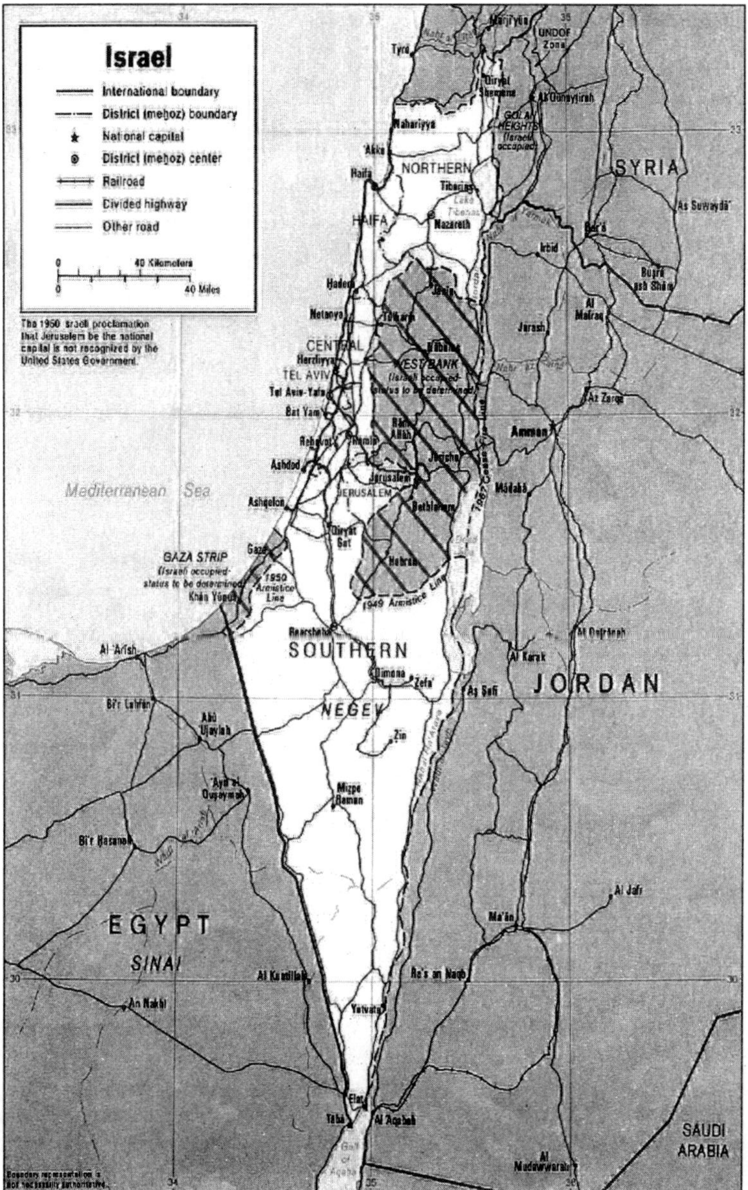

Sketch No.2: **Location of Israel**

Source: Internet : Google search engine

MAP NOT TO SCALE

5.2 Afghanistan

Afghanistan is a country with whom India have cordial relation since the ancient period till today except an era of "Taliban regime". Afghanistan is one of land locked states with an area of 7 lakh sq.kms. It is bounded by Russia in the North, Iran in the west and Pakistan and China in the east. It is one of the backward countries, of terrain with no adequate development to take place. Terrain is very difficult as it is covered by high altitude peaks, valley, caves etc. This territory of Afghanistan is 1,220 meters high from sea level. Helmand is the major river of Afghanistan. *(please see sketch no.3)*

The ratio of literacy is poor and by religion the majority of population is Sunni Muslims. Afghan society is feudal and tribal and dominated by the Mullahs and tribal sardars. Afghan tribesman is a natural soldier and has faced "defeat and victory" consecutively from the invasion of Alexander in 325 B.C. and the recent victory of the Americans against the Taliban regime.

The British had considered Afghanistan as the gateway to India and assiduously cultivated her as buffer states as the west also opens a route to Iran and to the Middle East. The well-known "Durand Line" lies between Afghanistan and Pakistan. Afghanistan is always subject to super power politics—due to its location and physical contiguity with Pakistan, China, Iran and Russia. It is possible for Russia to have an access to Arabian sea, Persian gulfs, Middle east via Afghanistan and Pakistan.

In view of the location and strategic importance of Afghanistan it is the subject of global strategy, directly and indirectly. Even in the past for longer period Afghanistan had acted as a "Buffer State" between British India and Czarist Russia.[6] Though it is poor in terms of Industrialisation and ratio of fertile soil is inadequate, certain minerals are found in plenty e.g. petrol, gold, silver in Afghanistan. It is a matter of remorse that the land of Afghanistan was a centre for:

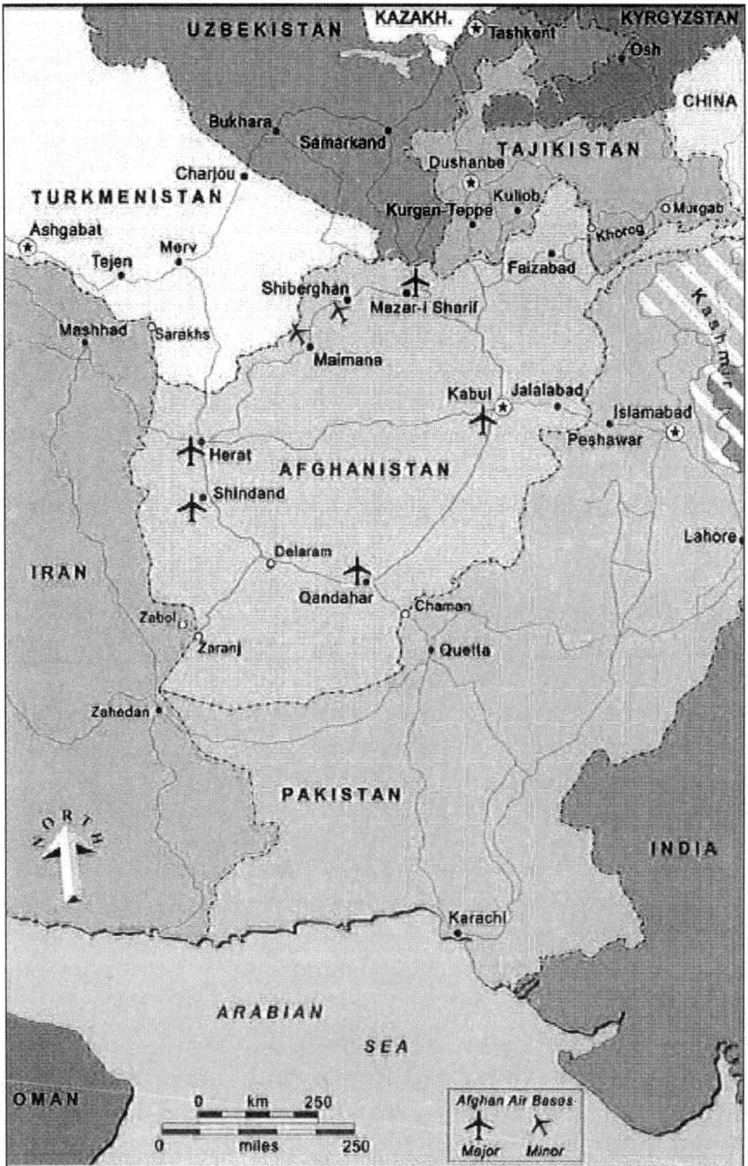

Sketch No.3: **Afghanistan**

Source : Internet : Google Search Engine

MAP NOT TO SCALE

1. Sponsoring Terrorism
2. Cultivation of opium

On account of its location, position and significance, every super power has ambitions to dominate Afghanistan as the puppet regime.

Therefore, it has been a subject of political instability and direct or indirect intervention or interference from time to time. It was the USSR who had intervened in Afghanistan in 1979. Then it became a centre of power politics and it was the USA who had appreciated Osama bin Laden as a great freedom fighter as he had fought against the USSR forces in Afghanistan. After the withdrawal of USSR forces from Afghanistan, in 1999 it was taken over by the Talibans and they established their own government.

Afghanistan became a "headquarter" for global terrorism and cultivation of poppy-narcotics—opium drugs. The United States of America has dismantled the terrorist training centers and thrashed out the Taliban regime from Afghanistan, by use of force.[7] In view of Unipolar World System, it may happen that the Americans' presence directly or indirectly will remain in Afghanistan.

5.3 Kuwait

Once upon a time Kuwait was a part of Ottoman Turkish Empire. Then it became a subject of mandate by British Administration on behalf of the League of Nations. British mandate came to an end in 1932 and after a lot of political "upheavels", Kuwait acquired independence in 1961.

Kuwait is the buffer state, which has been bounded by Iraq, Iran, Saudi Arabia and Persian Gulf *(sketch no.4)*. This territory does not receive adequate rainfall and hence one cannot find the required food, resources and adequate sources of water. On account of its geographical setting, water required for vegetation, flora and fauna are not available.[8] This territory has no other resources excest oil. Most of the land is arid desert and therefore, dependent on outside world for a number of things.

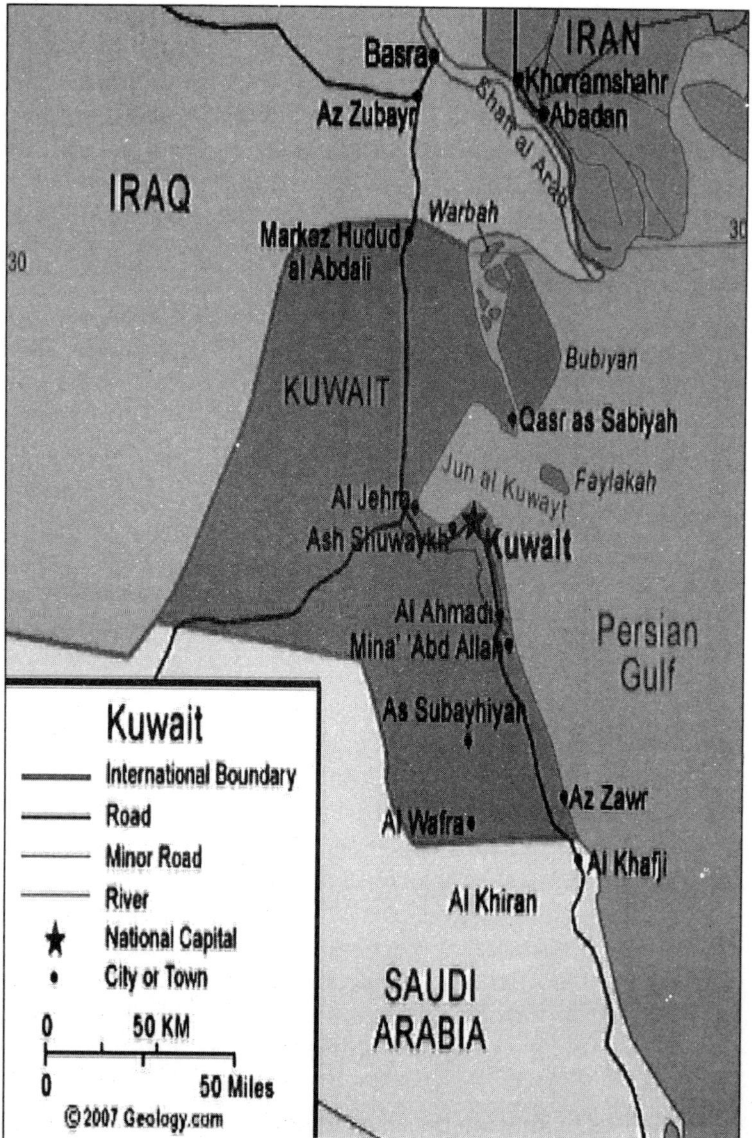

Sketch No.4: **Kuwait**

Source : Internet : Google search engine

MAP NOT TO SCALE

"Kuwait" came up in international focus only when Saddam Hussain, the then supremo of Iraq, sent his forces in 1990. On the basis of historical legacy Hon'ble Saddam Hussain claimed that it was a part of Iraq and it should be with Iraq only and as a result it was grabbed by Iraqi forces. It is needless to mention that the Iraqis were interested in the vast oil fields of Kuwait. Kuwait is one of the rich territories in terms of oil and natural gas. Out of world's oil deposits, Kuwait alone possesses 16.5 per cent of oil deposits. Oil refinery is situated at Meena-al-Ahmedi and the rights of this oil refinery company are reserved with America, Japan, United Kingdom, France etc. It is Kuwait that exports oil to the world, specially UK, USA, Japan, India and Australia.[9]

It was in Jan-Feb 1991 that the USA had sent her forces to Kuwait and at last US and her allied forces thrashed out the Iraqi forces from Kuwait. And it is well-known that America wanted to protect her political and economic interest only.

5.4 Siachen Glacier

Siachen Glacier is a new area of conflict since late 70's. Basically Siachen means "Garden of roses". But unfortunately and more so ironically it is now the highest battlefield on the globe. The Siachen Glacier is 76.4 kms long and 2.8 kms wide—the second largest glacier in the world outside the polar region. An area of Siachen Glacier receives a snowfall throughout the year and remains snowbound with extreme subzero temperature. During winter, temperature goes down to (minus) -55 degree centigrade and during summer (minus) -15 degree.[10] *(sketch no. 6).*

The seeds of this Siachen issue are contained in an agreement signed on 27th July 1949 and cease-fire line was determined at Karachi between India and Pakistan. The CFL was delineated upto Map point NJ 9842. The commission which was assigned the task to decide CFL could not be delineated beyond the point of NJ 9842 and the reason was the critical geographical conditions. An area beyond the NJ

9842 was considered "inaccessible" and critical for survival for human beings. Even during 1965 and 1971 wars this Siachen glacier area was not the subject of "battlefield" by any means. Siachen Glacier area came into focus when the mountaineers had conducted an expedition in this area and afterward published the maps in journals and showed the Siachen glacier as a Pakistani territory. So Pakistan encouraged the mountaineers from America and her Allies to launch expeditions and created an impression that this Glaciers belonged to Pakistan. India played a role like a "Master of Strategy" before Pakistan moved; India occupied the dominating heights and important passes on the saltors ridge line. This "Master stroke of Strategy" had a code name "Operation Meghdoot". In this very way Indian army proved its superiority over the adversary.[11]

From 1984 the world has witnessed that how the determined armed forces can perform their "duty" at the highest battle ground. There were two enemies in this Siachen glacier area—the first one is nature which is very cruel—Rough-Tough—and the other is the opponent forces. Nature does not permit human beings to survive easily. Heights of these glaciers are 18,000 to 22,000 feets from sea level. Survival at these heights and in such a critical condition, it requires physical fitness, strong determination and will-power. This is a glaring example of political expediency in the sacrifice of human lives.

5.4.1 Geostrategic Perspective

Siachen glacier is virtually the root of Eurasia and is surrounded by Pakistan-occupied Kashmir, India, Russia, China. All these territories are visible from the heights above 6080 meters subject to clear climate. To the east there is Aksai Chin, which was being illegally occupied by China during 1954-62. This Aksai Chin being occupied by China was a part of Indian Ladakh. To the west of this region the two towns of Pakistan occupied-Kashmir are situated i.e. Gilgit and Skardu. The terrain is inhospitable and financially it is useless. Even a single blade of grass does not grow in this area; in spite of this, both the entities stood firmly.

Indian armed forces have established undisputed sway over more than 2/3rd area of Siachen glacier and are able to control the major strategic passes and heights of the glacier. India enjoys a strategic consideration by virtue of its position. By occupying 2/3rd area of Siachen glacier India enjoys the following advantages:

1. Nubra valley which can pose a threat to Leh — a capital of Ladakh — and this area is surrounded by China. Because of the presence of Indian troops over there, India is able to prevent any possible movement by Pakistani army or terrorists through the Nubra valley to Leh. Therefore, Ladakh is free from terrorist activities as compared to Kashmir valley.
2. By virtue of India's position, it is possible to thwart potentially dangerous movements along the KaraKoram highway which would emanate from either China or Pakistan. India should not deny the possibility of joint venture by China and Pakistan against India. Therefore, holding of an area of Siachen is a matter of great importance for India. But both the countries of Pakistan and China do not want the presence of Indian troops over there.
3. Both India and Pakistan could save their time, manpower and resources, if they could withdraw from this area. But it requires goodwill, trust, and confidence at bilateral level and supported by material facts and previous experience. Indian Prime Minister Dr. Manmohan Singh expressed his desire that "Siachen glacier would be a mountain of peace". This will be decided by the future, so let's hope for the best.

5.5 Geostrategic Importance of Islands

Basically 'Island' means a piece or pieces of land which are surrounded by water. It is the piece of land not large enough to be called a continent. According to geographical description there were four types of Islands, coastal, located on continental shelf, inland seas and oceanic Islands.

"Location" of the Island is a deciding factor in relation to its significance in global strategy or "Power Politics". It is the Island which provides a support to combat forces by availing the oil, refuel, water... workshop facilities etc. It is the Island which has inter-relationship with the large part of the maritime activities in the ocean. In view of the significance of the Islands, grabbing of Islands often occurred and even war was fought to capture the Islands. Falkland war between Britain and Argentina is a good example.

5.5.1 Diego Garcia

The Indian Ocean is the only ocean named after a country as more than half of the people living on its shores are Indian. It is the third largest ocean in the world comprising more than 128 million square miles — an area where one-third of the human race resides here. There are 36 littoral and hinterland states embracing the stretch of the Indian Ocean.[13] *(sketch no.10).*

Diego Garcia Islands are located at the centre of the Indian Ocean. It is situated at the half way between eastern Africa and the Middle East. This Island is equidistant from all points. It is 1200 miles distant from the north-west of Mauritius, about 700 miles from south-east of Colombo and 1000 miles south-east of Kanyakumari. It is the place from where the Americans can keep an eagle's eye on the countries of the region. Diego Garcia has a good harbour and site for large airfield. Approximately, it is an area about 65 to 67 hundred acres. Diego Garcia is a part of changes; Archipelago consists of four Islands — Aldabra, Farquhar, Desrouches and Diego Garcia. Diego Garcia was handed over to the U.S.A by U.K.—the agreement and idea was for "joint use". So America established her naval base at Diego Garcia and declared ***"to fill-up a gap in the world-wide U.S. Naval Communication System"***. The U.S. Government spent millions of rupees to convert this Island into a "Military Base". Now there are lots of strategic advantages which are being enjoyed by U.S.A. Strategic considerations are as follows:-

a) By virtue of this Diego Garcia Islands, the U.S. could establish the link between her global defence communication network and Pentagon.

b) Communication can be maintained with the U.S. submarines, operating in Indian oceans and other centers of communication and information.

c) The U.S. can ensure the security and supply of oil, while exploiting the resources and man power at minimum cost in Africa and Asia.

d) To intervene in regional conflicts wherever and whenever the Americans interest would be disturbed. During Indo-Pak war of 1971 if America had a military base at Diego Garcia Island, then the result of this war would have been different.

e) Maintaining her presence in this region is to keep under pressure all littoral countries of Indian Ocean, and at the same time to check the Chinese influence.[14] This Island is feasible for attending the intended goal of U.S. policies, in Asia and Africa

Most of the littoral and hinterland states of Indian Ocean are alarmed at the development in this region for naval supremacy and anxious about their "security". By virtue of centric-Geostrategic location of Diego Garcia, America is enjoying strategic advantages. From strategic point of view it has vital importance for America. After all it is proved as a good point for the observation of a naval base and centre of marine transport for them.

5.5.2 Andaman Nicobar and Lakshadweep Islands (sketch no. 10)

In view of India's position as a dominant power in South Asian region India must be able to project her image in this region. And as such to maintain her image as a dominant power, she should have potential to go beyond her borders. India is trying to maintain it. For example, the role of IPKF in Sri Lanka, Maldives, and the incidence of landing of Indian troops at Chittagaon in 1971. These examples are enough to understand India's ambition "to be the hegemonic power of the south Asian region".

India's Maritime boundaries i.e. sea Coast, exclusive economic zone, territorial waters has a crucial part of her security management. In view of the super power rivalry in Indian Ocean and security of her maritime boundaries, the Andaman Nicobar and Lakshadweep Islands have a great significance. India had historical association with these Islands. During colonial period it was a place for punishment to the Indian revolutionaries and the freedom fighters. Mr. V. D. Sawarkar was imprisoned in the Cellular prison. He was the person who had visualised the significance of Andaman and Nicobar Islands and stated:-

"Andaman and Nicobar Islands is a nose of Indian Sub-continent."

Andaman and Nicobar Islands are comprised of over 300 Islands (1/10 are inhabited) with an area of 8,493 square miles spread over the length of 750 kms in the Bay of Bengal. Port Blair is the capital of Andaman and Nicobar Islands. It is 1255 kms away from Calcutta, 1100 kms from Chennai (Madras) and 1200 kms from Vishakapatnam. Port Blair has a natural harbour. Terrain is very difficult to access, and is occupied by altitudes and forest that are inhabited by various tribes. Andaman and Nicobar islands are of scattered nature and their population makes it difficult to illegal entries, as outsider can be identified immediately.

Geostrategic consideration for India:

1. It offers an adequate depth to "sea defence" from the east.
2. Strategically world vital link between India and Pacific Ocean can be controlled from these Islands. Even it has feasible access to Malacca Strait.
3. There, Islands can act as "air base" to extend Indian influence into South China Sea and even into South East Asian countries.
4. These Islands can act like "Aircraft Carrier" and dominate vital sea routes to Bangladesh, Myanmar

and even other International waterways. It can be a junction (link) between the Pacific and the Indian Ocean.

5. These Islands are most important from the strategic point of view:

5.1 Natural gas, oil and coal, gypsum, sulpher, timbers are available.

5.2 The sea is rich in marine life.

5.3 Excellent potential of petroleum.

5.4 These Islands have excellent potential for coffee, coco, spices, and plantation.

6. It's the "Heart" of the Bay of Bengal and is the natural gateway to Indian continent from the east.
7. It has centric position in the trade routes between the Indian Ocean and the Western countries operating via Suez Canal.
8. India can develop these Islands to meet the strategic requirements. This "Base" should be capable to face any maritime attack from the east. In view of super power rivalry in the Indian Ocean and Chinese Maritime strategy, it would be in India's interest that she should strengthen her position in these Islands. [15]

5.6 Lakshadweep Islands

The Lakshadweep Islands are similar to other coral Islands of the Indian ocean like Seychelles, Mauritius. The Lakshadweep islands are located in the Arabian Sea and comprise 36 Islands; these Islands are approximately 200 km away from Kerala sea coast. It has a crescent shape, extended in 29 sq. kms territory along the hills and dense forest.

Lakshadweep Islands are inhabited by Agatti, Ameni, Andrott and Bitra. And maximum population consists of Sunni Muslims.

As to the accessibility, it can be through ships, helicopters, and aircrafts etc. Agatti has good network of airfield. In view of Pakistan's Karachi port which is located in Arabian Sea, India should strengthen her position along with sophisticated weapons and equipments and required infrastructure at Lakshadweep Islands. From the Lakshadweep Island "Watch" can be kept on various routes which goes towards Suez canal, Cape of Iran etc.

Before India was a colony, it was the colonial powers that had arrived at the Lakshadweep Islands. By that time if the contemporary ruler had a strong Naval base over there then it could have been difficult for the colonial powers to invade India. On account of Pakistan's maritime strategy and their growing ties with the Chinese navy, it is highly essential for India to be "vigilant" and prepared for her strong defence at these Islands in the Arabian Sea.[16]

5.7 Antarctica

Antarctica is the coldest, driest, windiest and the most remote place on this earth. The environment of this area is unfriendly and poses a number of challenges. But it has a scope for natural resources, different species of beautiful animals in extreme climatic conditions. Antarctica is 14 million square kilometers in size and more than 98% of the area is permanently ice-covered. Ice is a great reservoir of water as 90% of it is fresh water. Antarctica has great potentials for mineral and marine resources. It is a continent surrounded by ocean while the Artic is an ocean almost surrounded by continents and Greenland.[17] **(*sketch no.*5).**

5.7.1 Land and Resources

The Antarctica region is highly rich in terms of minerals and energy sources. According to the study of Geologists, variety of minerals and energy resources can be found such as nickel, platinum, copper, chromium, zinc, cobalt, gold, tin, uranium and coal. According to Gulf Oil Company "there could be about 50 billion barrels or even more oil in Antarctica". The U.S. geologists also agreed and concluded that the entire continent may have good major mineral deposits. Oil is yet to be discovered but strong evidences indicate its existence. All these natural assets have to be

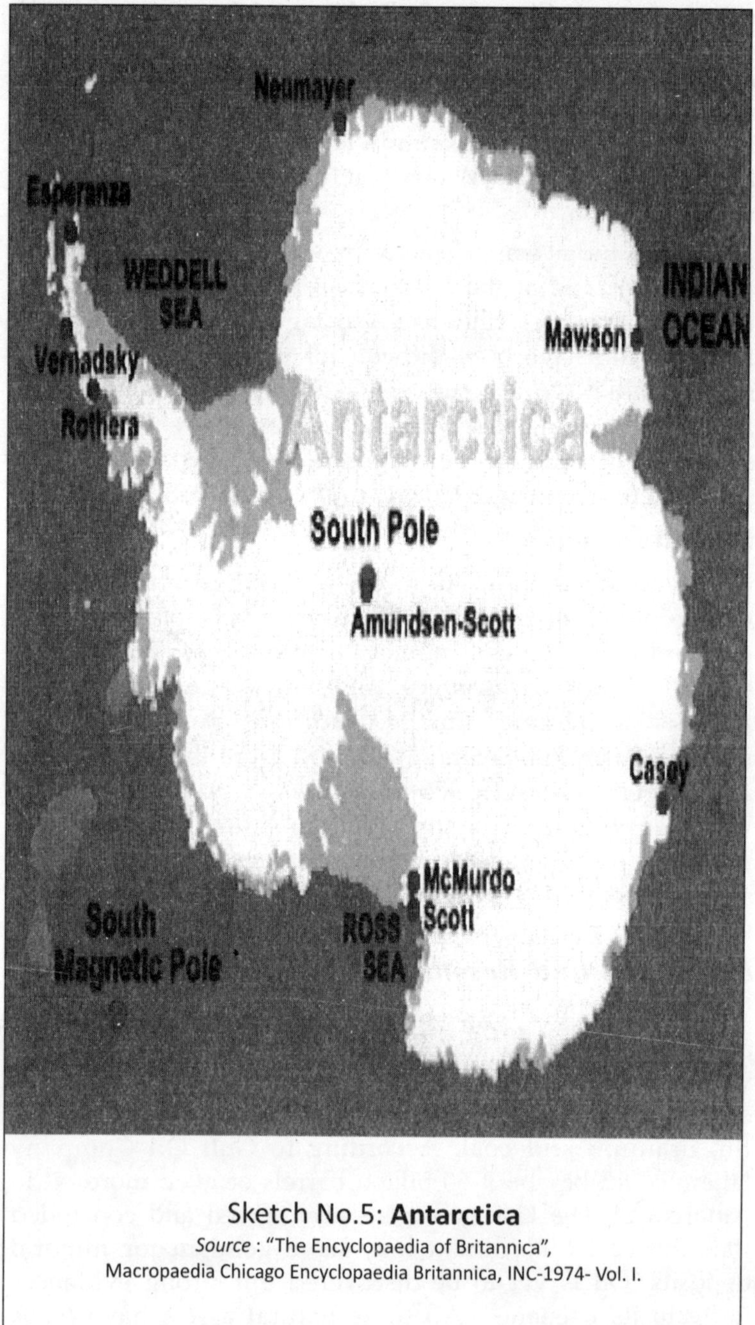

Sketch No.5: **Antarctica**

Source : "The Encyclopaedia of Britannica",
Macropaedia Chicago Encyclopaedia Britannica, INC-1974- Vol. I.

MAP NOT TO SCALE

explored and a legal, political and economic framework should be devised in order to protect the environment. The interested and the claimant countries may get tangled in eco-military-political tension as the resources are subjects of sovereignty. The issue of exploration and exploitation would be the centre of conflict.[18]

5.7.2 Strategic Importance

As regards the richness of this region in terms of minerals, marine and energy resources, the major western European powers had already occupied the position and claimed their sovereignty. The sovereignty claims made by the seven countries i.e. Argentina, Chile, France, Australia, Norway, Newzealand and Great Britain, are overlapping each other's sectors and therefore denying each other's sovereignty claim. The third world countries do not want to allow these seven countries to take the privilege of their positions in Antarctica and therefore tried to pass the resolution in UN on CHM. Antarctica region is to be recognised as a 'Common Heritage of Mankind' i.e. share management in the common area. It should be used for peaceful purposes or scientific and environmental research. But due to vested interests of the concerned powers, except few amendments in Antarctic treaty system, nothing could happen regarding reorganisation of Antarctica region to be a CHM. Regarding conflict between developed and developing countries for allocation and availing of resources of Antarctica, some flexibility and spirit of accommodation is shown by these powers and some of the developing countries like India became a member of treaty body i.e. Antarctica club.

Antarctica was discovered by these seven countries: France, Chile, Argentina, Newzealand, Australia, Norway and Great Britain and have claimed their sovereignty over this region. It is deeply freezed by ATS—Antarctica Treaty System. Antarctica is strategically important for the world and specially the claimant countries. It is needless to mention that if the vast deposits of minerals and resources are exploited, it will be a great help to the countries and specifically to third world countries which are in the pursuit of development. If anybody, despite costly and environmental barriers exploited the "resources" another question could arise and that is regarding share or allocation. And in this context there may be discrimination between A.T.S. and the rest of international community. Such discrimination may lead to "conflict". [20] The tourists have been attracted by this region but due to some uncertainties it is yet to take shape. People have heard and read about the wonders of this region. Tourism would be one of the potential sources of income but subject to governing factors alongwith sophisticated means and infrastructure.

5.7.3 Wonder

The Antarctica region is the only place on the earth where peace exists and Nations-States are working together for the scientific research. And the place where concept of "frontier" exists is Antarctica region and ocean it is being vanished from the land. This region is practically a first "Nuclear Free Zone" where the nuclear program is banned. The USA and Russia have Scientific Lab (station) at South Geographic pole and south Geomagnetic pole. The location of scientific stations of the super powers indicates "monopoly". The "location" of scientific station of the super power is feasible, the temperature is less critical than the other parts of the Antarctica. The countries which joined the Antarctica treaty later had to obtain the permission from claimant states and then establish their bases (Lab). This mainland of Antarctica was used by Germany during World War II [21].

5.7.4 India's Concerned

The year of 1980 was a landmark for India, as India was included in the ATS i.e. Antarctica Treaty system. To carry out all activities in Antarctica, the Department of Ocean Development was established in July 1981 at New Delhi (India). Since 1981 to 2001, India launched 21 expeditions. On 6th December 1981 the first scientific expedition was launched to Antarctica which was led by Dr. S. S. Qasim. They reached after 33 days. This first expedition was named as 'Operation Gangotri'. The permanent scientific station was built within two months, named Dakshin Gangottri, located at latitude $70^{0}05$ and longitude $12^{0}00^{1}$ E in Antarctica. Another research centre settled by India, is named "Maitri".[22]

Peninsular India and Antarctica were the parts of Gondwanaland and the Ocean is the only access for India to reach over there. India has a vast coastline for fishing and also for other water resources. Our object is to promote scientific research and its relevant studies. In 1983 India got sanction of consultative status by article 13 of Antarctica treaty. India has already established two scientific stations while enjoying the consultative status given by ATS. [23] Over and above, the fact cannot be denied that India is the country whose population has crossed 110 crores. In view of this largest population India needs maximum resources and minerals through various sources and Antarctica is the potential land of the resources. In future if the political compromise takes place, the resources of Antarctica would be exploited and India will be benefited. In such circumstances India would like to have a fair share in it.

Footnotes

1. Bharat Bhusan Gupta, *Arab Israeli Relations,* Ashish Publishing House, New Delhi, 1978, p.4.
2. *Ibid.*, p.6
3. Lt. Col. Banerjee & Major Anil Athale, *Arab Israeli wars 1967 & 1973,* T.S. Press, Calcutta, India, 1980, pp.11-13.
4. Mark A. Heller, *A Palestine State: The Implication for Israel* Haward University Press, Britain, 1983, p.217.
5. K.P. Misra, *Afghanistan in Crisis,* Vikas Publication, Ghaziabad, U.P. 1981, p.13.
6. M.P. Srivastava, *Soviet Intervention in Afghanistan,* Ashoka Press, New Delhi, 1980, p.66.

7. *Maharashtra Times*, Marathi Edition, Mumbai, 8th Oct 2001, Editorial Page and Headlines *see also* Ahmed Rashid, Taliban: The story of Afghan warlords, London, Pan Books; Pan Macmilan Ltd; 2001, pp.7-10.
8. Bruce W. Watson, *Military Lessons of The Gulf War* Lancer International, New Delhi, 1991, pp.1-4.
9. Cattrey Matt and Chadwick Frank, *Gulf War Fact Book*, Jupiter Publication, New Delhi, 1991, pp. 22-24.
10. Capt. Ahlawat S.S., "The Saichen Impasse", *Indian Defence Review*, Lancer International, New Delhi, 1988, July. Pp.85-86.
11. Prof. A.P. Chaudhary and others, *Military Geography*, Nirali Prakashan, Pune, 1995, pp. 275-76.
12. Chacko Arun, "Siachen Glacier" *Indian Express* , Mumbai, 15th Nov 1987.
13. Anand Mathur, "Growing Importance of the Indian Ocean in post cold war era and its implication for India" *Strategic Analysis*, Vol.26, No. 4, Oct-Dec 2002,. pp. 550-551, I.D.S.A. New Delhi.
14. Prof. S. R.Latkar and A.S. Apte, *Political Geography*, Vidya Prakashan, Nagpur, 1998, pp.. 109-113. *See also* Rodney W. Jones, "U. S. Interest in the Indian Ocean Region", *Indian Journal of Defence studies special issue on Indian Ocean*, Vol. 12, Department of Defence Studies, University of Allahabad 1983, pp.41-50.
15. Prof. S.R. Latkar and A.S. Apte, *op. cit*. pp. 119-121.
16. Dr. R.N.Mishra, *Indian Ocean and India's Security*, Mittal Publication, New Delhi, 1986 pp. 25-27.
17. Edward and Steven, "Latin America and Antarctica", *Current History* Vol.82, Philadelphia, Nov-Feb 1983, pp. 89-90.
18. Stonehouse Barnard Phillips, *Illustrated Atlas of the World*, London, George Phillip and Sons Ltd. 1982, p. 174.
19. The New Encyclopaedia of Britannica Macropaedia, Chicago Encyclopedia Britanica INC, 1974, Vol. I p.965.
20. Satya, Sharma, *Breaking The Ice In Antarctica; The First Indian Wintering In Antarctica*. New Age International Ltd, 2001, New Delhi, p.8.

21. R.C. Sharma, Editor, *Growing Focus on Antarctica*, Rajesh Publication, 1968, New Delhi, p.215.
22. Sanjay, Chaturvedi, *Drawing of Antarctica: A Geopolitical Analysis*, Segment Book Publication, New Delhi, 1990, pp. 163-164.
23. R.C., Sharma, *op. cit.*, p. 252.

❖ ❖ ❖

6

STRATEGIC MINERALS AND RESOURCES

6.1 INTRODUCTION

"Strategic Minerals"—the term has become more and more generalised affer it was originated during World War I. It was "France" which had acquired Alsace & Lorraine territory by the Germany as a part of treaty of Versailles signed at the end of World War I. Even Freidrich Ratzel, the well-known Geopolitician, while explaining the laws of the growth of a state had emphasised that statesmen must acquire "Political Valuable" area that means rich and fertile area. "Territory" would not be considered as an essential element for forming up a state unless the particular chunk of territory possesses adequate minerals and resources.[1] Strategic minerals does not mean only mine resources, it has to be considered in a wider context—minerals, resources, and even raw materials.

It is very difficult to categorise the strategic and non-strategic minerals. The term "strategic" is used in a wider sense. Strategic minerals are useful not only for production of war materials, but also vital to strengthen the position of a country in every respect. In "modern warfare" country's war potential is based on available resources and raw material with it. And it is one of the crucial elements of National Power. The "resources" have a crucial role in industrial and economic development and in defence preparedness of the country. These strategic minerals which are highly essential are not easily available and if at all they are available then they would be available in inadequate quantity. The minerals which help to strengthen the security, by exploiting and using it, are, for example, uranium, coal, natural gas, oil, steel etc. Uranium is essential to produce Nuclear energy. Without it production of nuclear energy is not possible. And no country can afford easily to produce Nuclear energy by using platinum. It is to be noted that denial of the resources is one of the most important aspects of a grand strategy and at the same time it should be ensured that supply and security of strategic minerals must be maintained.[2] It has to be mentioned that "Geopolitics" deals with inequality in terms of allocation of the resources by nature. Having strategic minerals and resources is the pre-requisite to attain the status of super power or to attain the Industrial and economic development of the country. The national power of a country is mainly determined on the basis of Industrial and military power. No nation can develop industrially and militarily unless it possesses sufficient strategic minerals and resources.

Extensive natural resources and minerals and supplies of raw materials are indispensable for political-military power. It is highly vital for a country to emerge as a powerful country like China who has utilised all "Minerals and Resources". It was possible for China to emerge as a powerful nation only due to availability of minerals and resources within the country. The goods and commodities being produced by available minerals and resources are most valuable for a sound economy. Today is the age of machine which produces weapons, equipments, tools, building materials and it is possible, only if you have strategic minerals and resources.

6.2 Types of Minerals

Every country has its own planning, programming and ambitions. And, therefore, minerals and resources are to be made available. The requirements may change according to the circumstances and priorities. There were three types of requirements of resources i.e. "essential", "strategic" and "critical".

1) **Essential:** For the process of nation building and development, certain minerals and raw materials are highly essential. Without such minerals or resources a country cannot carry out the process of development. Even such essential materials are vital for war economy, for example, coal, gold, oil, silver, iron etc. are very vital.

2) **Strategic:** The minerals and resources are highly essential to strengthen the war economy and also vital for war material production but are not easily available and if at all, they may not be able to satisfy the demands.

3) **Critical:** The minerals which are required for war economy but their supplies of domestic origin are inadequate as per demand and are as critical like oil, lead, copper, gold, platinum etc. [3]

It is a primary responsibility of every Government to adopt a number of measures to ensure the "supply and availability" of strategic minerals and resources without any obstruction. It may happen that during emergency the Government may not be able to make available required minerals and resources. In such a case there are two options:

1. By studying the future possibilities required minerals and resources have to be spared and dumped. It requires foresight and strategic approach.
2. To find out the substitute material may be synthetic/artificial. It depends on how the Government can tackle the situation.[4]

6.3 Uses of Strategic Minerals and Resources

Natural Resources: Minerals are a gift given by nature which cannot be produced by human efforts. It is explored and then may be exploited by technological know-how, capital investment and skilled man-power. And the raw materials that can be produced by human efforts are—rubber, timber, teakwood, gum etc. Some of the minerals and resources are so vital that without them weapons, equipments, materials and the infrastructure cannot be produced. The following table shows the uses of resources.

S. No.	Name of the Strategic Minerals and Resources	Uses for production of
1.	Tungsten	Nuclear submarine.
2.	Uranium and Platinum	Nuclear energy, weapons and various peaceful purposes.
3.	Cobalt	Space technology.
4.	Zinc	Ship coating and galvanised iron sheets.
5.	Graphite	Aircraft production.
6.	Iron(steel)	Weapons, vehicles, tools, machinery, equipments
7.	Diamond	Drill machine, cutting tools, blade, cutter etc and jewellery
8.	Copper	Electrification
9.	Coal, Natural gas, Oil, Petroleum	Energy production - Industry, transport, cooking etc.
10.	Thorium, Vanadium and Molyblenum Uranium (Atomic Minerals)	Production of Atomic power, Nuclear weapons and fuel for rockets.
11.	Manganese	Industry- Metallurgy. Dry battery and melting process etc.
12.	Mica	Battleships, Telegraphy, Telephone, Aircrafts and wireless installation etc.
13.	Sliver, Gold and Bauxite	Domination in Economic and Political field.

S. No.	Name of the Strategic Minerals and Resources	Uses for production of
14.	Aluminium	Aircrafts, vehicles, Railways compartment, Electric machinery etc.
15.	Rubber	All types of Tube, tyres and jungle shoe
16.	Timber/Teakwood	Weapons-equipments, furniture, ship building etc.
17.	Food	Survival of human beings and even animals
18.	Water	Survival of every organism – human, animals, vegetation.
19.	Cotton	All types of clothings.
20.	Flora, Fauna and Vegetation	Medicine, leather, food etc. [5]

During World War II the minerals and resources had a great significance for the conduct of war. The minerals and resources were used with economy and foresight and to make it clear, the list of strategic minerals was published in 1941 by U.S. President Roosevelt. And strategic minerals were defined as follows:-

> *"Those minerals essential is used in war emergency the procurement of which is in inadequate quantities, quality and time is sufficiently uncertain for any reason to require prior provision for the supply thereof".*

It was the Allies who had visualised the significance of minerals and distinguish between strategic and non-strategic materials. And as a result of it during World War II Air Force of allies (US and UK) had carried out the strategic bombing in deep territory of Germany. This strategic bombing was targeted against industries' iron and coal mines, oil deposits of Germany, in order to cripple her war potential. So, in this way the minerals and resources have a great significance.

6.4 Importance of Oil-Petroleum

Oil even today is considered a cheap and basic source of energy. Petrol, diesel, kerosene are the sub-products of petroleum and basically they are being used for energy production and as a fuel for vehicles. The overall development of a country also depends upon available sources of energy and network of transportation. No nation can attain the status of a "developed" country without "industrial development" and it cannot be attained without the constant flow and stockpile of petroleum. Oil has become essential in modern technical societies and is the lifeblood of modern mobile armed forces. It is to be considered that energy sources are fundamental to nation's potency. The Governments of respective countries must control its energy resources as well as discover the new sources of energy, including stockpile of adequate reserves, and ensure that owing to lack of petroleum the national life is not jeopardised.

6.4.1 Significance

In modern society "oil" has occupied a significant place in "National Life". Without adequate "Reserve" no country can even think about to conduct war. Without sufficient stocking of oil conduct of war is likely to be impossible. All movements of combat forces i.e. Tank, APC, Aircrafts, Submarine, Vehicles, Ships depend on fuel resources and its supply. Therefore, oil has been called the "Blood Stream of Modern War" on the battle front and even on the domestic front; both depend upon oil. The industrial and economic development of a country is determined by energy sources and petroleum products which have occupied a significant place in the modern world.

As regards oilfields and oil deposits, the west Asia-Persian Gulf including Middle East is rich as compared to other parts of the globe. This territory is like a land bridge between Australia, Africa and Asia. The well-known Suez Canal is also located in this region. And out of global deposits 60% of oil deposits are in this area. Saudi Arabia, Kuwait,

Iraq, Iran, Jordan, Oman, Bahrain, Syria, Egypt, Israel, and Turkey are known as oil producing countries. [6] These countries are exporting petroleum products—oil—to the various countries. Oil and its by-products are vital not only as fuel but also are used as other activities affecting everyday life. To maintain the continuity in Economic Development, since post world war second era, the western countries have been using oil as a main instrument. Even "World's Economy" revolves around the oil business industries. Oil being non-renewable resources is likely to diminish substantially by A.D. 2030.[7]

6.4.2 Super Power's Interest and Objectives

This oil product region is most important for a number of reasons.

1. Israel was called an agent of USA to check and counter Russian influence in the oil-producing region during cold war period.
2. The USA, UK, France and their allies invested crores of dollars in the oil refinery projects and earned the Petro Dollars.
3. Arab-Israel conflict is one of the points for escalation. Four major wars had been fought and even today despite their working for "peace", minor skirmishes are continued and it is very difficult to predict the future of Arab-Israel conflict.

   During war the exports of oil to the western countries were banned by the Arab countries and thereby causing loss to the western countries. This issue of Arab-Israel is very complicated, with relevance to Nationalism, Justice, Security and Territory.
4. This oil producing region is an emotional pull i.e. "Jerusalem". The Christians, Muslims and Jews have emotional attachment with this pilgrim centre. At Jerusalem Jews temple exists, which was built by Solomon and for the Christians it's a place of martyrdom of Jesus Christ. And for the Muslims it was the place from which Muslim Prophet Mohammad ascended the Heaven. [8]

Objectives of Super Powers:

1) To ensure the security of oil supply at a minimum cost to their home-state without any obstruction.
2) To maintain the pressure and political influence with a view to achieve their "national interest" from time to time.
3) To ensure the economic interest and earn the maximum amount of oil refinery projects.
4) And to sell the weapons and equipments and continue the earning of money.
5) To use the Suez Canal as a short-cut to establish the link with Mediterranean Sea and the Indian Ocean.[9]

6.4.3 Politics of Oil

In view of the significance and uses of oil—Petroleum products i.e. petrol, diesel, oil—everybody is trying to dominate and control this oil-producing region by hook or crook. In this region, especially the Americans are very much ambitious to control over this vast oil fields as well as OPEC (Organisation of Oil Producing and Exporting Countries). This was the reason why the the Americans fought the war against Iraq in 1990-91 and even thrash out Saddam Hussain from power. It is the U.S.A. who always pretends to be the leader of "Democratic World" and will not bear any violation of Freedom, Sovereignty, Security and Human rights. On this ground in 1990-91 the U.S.A. intervened with Iraq-Kuwait war on behalf of Kuwait and drove the Iraqi forces from Kuwait. Then on the same ground, can the Americans intervene with Tibet and expel the Chinese forces from Tibet. The answer is that Tibet is not "rich" by any means, like Kuwait.

The Americans and its allies don't want the oilfields of Saudi Arabia to be controlled by Al Qaeda whereby terrorism would be strengthened and thereby causing threat to the West. At present the Americans' priority is to control over Iraq with a view to exercise control over the oilfields of Middle East and West Asia. Instead of arresting Osama bin Laden dead or alive the Americans have concentrated on Iraq. [10] Needless to mention that "Oilfields of Kuwait" was the main reason for grabbing of Kuwait by Iraq in the nineties. And even Iraq-Iran fought the war during eighties to dominate the oil-rich region of "Shatt-Al-Arab". In view of the above facts it can be concluded that oil deposits are the blood streams of modern age/war. In future, Russian federation is going to dominate the oil diplomacy in the world as it is the second largest reservoir of oil.

6.5 Natural Gas

"Natural Gas" is one of the cheap sources of energy. It is a basic feature that is extremely clean and convenient to use. In terms of weight it is lighter than water and oil. It is found in the region of coal and petroleum. It mainly contains methane, ethane, propane and butane to the extent of 95%. It also contains nitrogen, carbon-dioxide, hydrogen-sulphide and helium in small amount. It occurs along with oil; many oil wells produce natural gas as a by-product. Most of the world's natural gas is produced in the U.S.A, Russia, Canada, Western Europe and Central Asian States. It is non-polluting and it can be used for various purposes.

In 1820 the U.S.A had used this natural gas as a source of energy for the first time. Now natural gas industries serve as highly visible global activities producing a product in high demand world-wide, but with limited source of supply. As compared to oil, the ratio of consumption of natural gas seems to be limited and it is difficult and risky for transportation.

Natural gas being a cheap source of energy is used for various purposes. It can be used as a fuel for (two or four wheeler) vehicles. This gas is cheaper than petrol or diesel and the common people also can afford it easily. For cooking purpose this (LPG) gas is being used as a substitute for stove and wood. It can be used for production of electricity, chemical fertilisers and ammunition.

In view of the utility and cost factor, natural gas like oil also has occupied a significant place and come up as one of the strategic sources of energy. Though gas is considered an economic product, if only the mining area is nearest to the market and the area should accommodate pipeline connections. This may be the reason why China started the construction of pipeline for importing gas from Kazakistan. The approximate cost of this pipeline is 18 Arab Dollars. [11]

India also has some deposits of Natural Gas. According to geological survey of India natural gas can be found in Gujarat, Orissa, Assam, Arunachal and Himachal Pradesh and even Rajasthan. In the late eighties natural gas was found in Mumbai high-sea and India has already started its use from Mumbai High. Through pipeline it is being dumped at Uran and from Uran it is supplied to the various industries and customers. [12]

In view of increasing population and consumption, India requires more and more "natural gas". Whatever "Deposits of Natural Gas" that India has are not adequate. Therefore, India is willing to construct the "pipelines" for importing natural gas from Iran as well as central Asian States. Construction of pipeline is costly and a hard business. But taking into consideration the vision of future, it is vital for India.

6.6 Water

Generally the basic needs of human beings are food, cloth and shelter but practically non-polluted air—Oxygen—and water are essential for every organism. Water is one of the essential things for life, without which survival is not possible. It should be remembered that "WATER" creates power by motion without being burnt like, coal, oil etc. Water is one of the major sources of "Power Production" through Hydropower plants, Hydel power project or wind mill, and power can be produced.

It is very strange that 80% of the earth surface is occupied by water and yet we are facing scarcity of water. It is difficult to believe this, but it's a fact and a bitter truth. There are lots of sources of water like rainfall, glaciers, rivers, lakes, damps, tube wells etc. But due to deforestation, increasing population, urbanisation and rapid industrialisation the "Ecological Balance" has been disturbed which ultimately resulted in melting of glaciers, drought or inadequate rainfall. Therefore "water scarcity" has come up as one of the major issues.[13] The Armed forces are very much aware of the significance of water. Especially during "Desert Warfare" the fighting goes on between two forces for hours and hours just to capture the "Water Well". Destruction of water storage of enemy also becomes an essential task of combat forces, during desert war.

In desert warfare it has been said that "blood is cheaper but water is costly". "Water" has played a very crucial role in industrial, agricultural, urban and economic development of the country. It is to be noted that in North America and Western Europe during Industrial revolution, "electricity" for machines was produced by power production projects. Even today it is the most important source to produce electricity in the third world countries. Numbers of countries are dependent on Hydropower project for electricity such as, Norway 99%, Switzerland 74% and Canada 57%. Agriculture, Industrial, Economic development of a country is dependent upon energy resources at minimum cost and "Water" is one of the most important sources of energy from the economic point of view.[14]

Never before "water" occupied such a significant place. In view of the increasing population in over-crowded cities, faulty water supply system, misuse of water, lack of proper water storage infrastructure and lack of tendency of finding more water sources have resulted in scarcity of water. The strategic importance of water is beyond doubt. It should be remembered that water is precious. It is to be used with economy, foresight and sparingly. "Conflict" for water will take place in this 21st century at domestic, regional and even at global level. And examples are Kaveri water dispute, dispute between Punjab and Haryana i.e. within Indian states and the Sindhu River, the Bhaglihar water distribution between India and Pakistan etc.

Footnotes

1. R.L. Dwivedi, *Fundamentals of Political Geography*, Chaitanya Publishing House, University Road, Allahabad, 1990, pp. 26-27.
2. Precis on *Strategic Minerals*, Department of Defence and Strategic Studies, University of Pune, Pune, 1982.
3. Sudeepta Adhikari, *Political Geography*, Rawat Publication, New Delhi, 2002, pp. 334-37.
4. Precis on *Strategic Minerals, op. cit.*, (D.D.S.S. Pune)
5. R.L. Dwivedi, 1998, *op.cit.*, pp. 0-91 *see also* Prof. A.P. Choudhary.

   Military Geography, Nirali Prakashan, Pune, 1995 pp. 79-82.
6. Prof. S. R. Latkar and A. S. Apate, *Political Geography*, Vaidhya Prakashan, Nagpur, 1998, .pp.22-24.
7. Maj. Gen. S. C. N. Jathar, *Everything is for Oil*, Pune Sakal, Pune, Dated-6th April 2003.
8. Anil Athale (Maj) and Banarjee, *Arab Israeli wars 1967 and 1973*, T.S. Press, Calcutta, India, 1980, pp. 13-14.
9. Maj. Gen. S.C.N. Jathar, *op. cit.*, 6/4/2003.
10. Arun Sadhu, "Why? For Oil", *Maharashtra Times*, Marathi Edition, Mumbai, 22/11/2003.
11. Majid Husain, Editor, "Resource Geography", Anmol Publication Pvt. Ltd., New Delhi, 2002, pp. 140-142.
12. Prof. A.P. Chaudhary and others, *Military Geography*, Nirali Prakashan, 1995, Pune, M.S., p. 130.
13. N.V. Pandari Konihan, Director, "Water Resources Development: Present and Future", Guest lecture/ Seminar paper, Centre for Resources and Ocean Development, Anna University, Madras, 600025, India. Oct 1995.
14. Majid Husian, *op. cit.*, 2006, pp. 84-86.

✤ ✤ ✤

7

MILITARY GEOGRAPHY

7.1 INTRODUCTION

"Military Geography" is one of the vital subjects for local field commander—without studying or understanding it, he cannot conduct any military operation. Military Geography has deep-rooted linkages with war and Geography. It is the discipline in which the study of relationship between war and Geography is being carried out. Not a single aspect of military operation—insurgency or anti-terrorist operation—would be completed without adequate knowledge of local geography. And hence it is being considered an academic discipline whose study is a pre-requisite for every military officer. In this discipline every geographical factor-size, structure of land, nature of terrain, climate, population etc. has relevance directly/indirectly to the conduct of war. Military Geography is an academic discipline which is popularised and has occupied a significant place in the 20th century. Now it is one of the vital disciplines to be studied by the policy and decision-makers of the respective countries.

4.2 Meaning, Concept and Definitions

According to Peltier and Percy: **"Military Geography means a study of application of 'Geographic Discipline' in order to conduct Military Operation."** This definition highlights that how and to what extent Geography has relevance to military operation. As Ranner explains:

"Military Geography means a strategy of Men, Space and Resources in relation to the conduct of war".

In this definition an attempt is made to focus how human beings can use location-position-environment for their intended goal i.e. for their successful conduct of war.

According to White and Ranner, Military Geography is a sub-division of Human Geography, specially concerned with "Earth-Man" relationship with a special kind of emphasis. It is not the relationship between physical environment and human groups of societies but the relationship between geographical factors and political entities. A well-known military person—General Wavel—during his North African Campaign—World War II—stated:-

"....it is the geography of a territory (battlefield) which decides the "Nature of Warfare".

The above statement is enough to understand the meaning, definition, principles and functions of military geography. Every battle has relevance to local geography. Every campaign, war, battle has a great concern with Military Geography. The conduct of war, defeat or victory depends on an understanding of Military Geography. According to German Professor Awal Bans, war is a geographical fact. Military Geography is a geography in which military activities are to be studied in relation to geographical facts of the situation. It is the study of the military values of geographical factors and it is, therefore, a legitimate projection and extension of political geography.

Military Geography is the study of military evaluation of geographical realities of political area i.e. state/nation, concerned with formation of its defence policy, war plans and actual conduct of combat operations. In other words, it is an analysis of area of operation from the strategic and tactical points of view—structure of land, nature of terrain, climate, natural hazards etc. It is an application of geographic discipline in order to conduct military operation.

Military Geography means a study which is concerned with places and regions, their properties and differences—both physical and social—and of the way in which the efficiency of military activities can be influenced by the above factors. [2] Geography is concerned with efficiency and the cost of military activities. Military Geography is considered a common and simple logic adopted for the consideration of national policy, international politics and the level of industrial and military technology and the actual facts of the situation. It means an interaction between geographical condition and military affairs. It focuses on the geometry of military situation and the effect on the location, characteristic and distribution of environment, peoples, forces and ultimately upon command decision. [3]

- **Elements of Military Geography:** Hence it is understood that Military Geography is the military evaluation of geographical realities of political area concerned with the formulation of its defence policies, war plans and the actual conduct of combat operation.[4] The geographical realities incorporate the aerial character i.e. physical, economic and human elements of the spatial environment of a State. Military Geography is concerned with establishment of requirement for training equipments and organisation of the Armed forces.

The geographical realities of political areas condition the characterisation of:

a) It's a "Military Doctrine" which in turn is a projection of national policies and postures.

b) It's a Grand Strategy which flows from the current Military Doctrine and envisages the most effective application of the entire war potential of the state.

c) It's the tactical and logistics operational plans for the most effective tackling of defence forces.[5]

4.3 Types of Military Geography

Taking into consideration the meaning, concept and elements of Military Geography in a wider perspective, it can be categorised on the basis of actual functions of it.

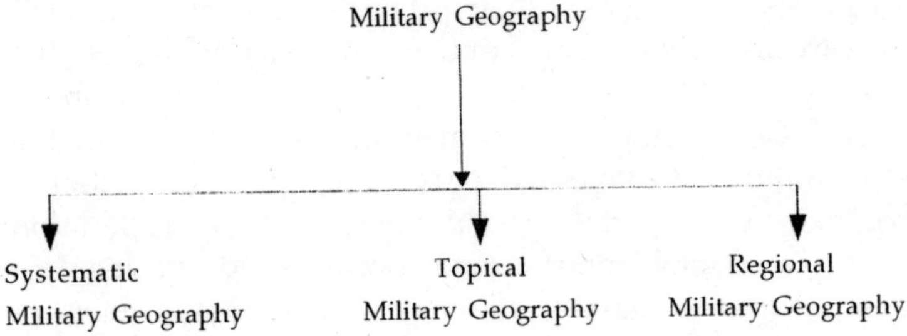

Systematic Military Geography signals the application of systematic science to the conduct of military affairs. Purely gamut of physical to social phases of geography i.e. Geomorphology and ethnography are encompassed. The Topical geography bridges the gap between systematic geography and military science. It includes the environmental aspects of National Power, engages in the design of material and penetrates environmental facets of the strategy tactics and logistics. This topical geography accounts for the differences in Doctrine imposed by different environment. The Regional geography acts as the synthesizer bringing together various aspects of geography. It resolves the problems by matching a known environment with the appropriate set of principles.[6]

7.4 Scope, Significance and Uses

Diplomats, Policy-Decision-makers and the top-level Military officers are the primary and practical users of Military Geography.

1. Every military operational planning requires the detail geographical knowledge of a battlefield. Every Military Commander must be aware of the geographical realities of the area of operation. Japanese attack on Burma—now Myanmar—during World War II is a bright example in this regard. The Japanese had adequate knowledge

of the facts of the situation. Therefore, they were able to jerk and surprise their enemy i.e. the British.

2. Military Geography helps in evaluating the national objective and capabilities at all levels in the pursuit of national interest. Thus the application of geographical science imparts to grand strategy—Strategy and Tactics—which has a great contribution to the success of military operation.
3. It is a Military Geography which dictates the nature of warfare, be it a desert, or jungle warfare or plain.
4. Military Geography is the determinant factor which determines the nature of defence preparedness of the country; for example, being a peninsular location, the defence preparedness of the U.K.–Britain—mainly consisted of "Naval Centric".
5. The knowledge of Military Geography is vital to determine the foreign as well as the defence policy of the country. Napoleon Bonaparte used to say that: "foreign policy can be determined by the geography". Neither foreign nor even defence policy can formulate without due consideration to Military Geography.
6. Military Geography has a great concern with strategic matters and affecting Grand Strategy, Strategy and Tactics. During war, sometime armed conflict continues to dominate or grab the strategic points. Indo-Pak conflicts in Siachen Glacier area is a distinct example in this context. Just for the sake of strategic benefits, consideration, both the countries deployed their "Forces" in this world's highest battlefield. It is very difficult to sustain the position at such a high, may the highest battlefield.
7. It is the Military Geography which restricts the enemy's movement and the history of warfare is a witness to it. During World War II, Hitler's Operation 'Barbarossa' was a failed one. German Army was unable to conquer

the Soviet Russia due to its large size, shape and severe winter.[7]

The calculations of Hitler failed and moreover he was unable to understand the scope and significance of Military geography of the U.S.S.R.

8. Military Geography provides the basis for the organisation and conduct of war. It provides detailed informations to R&D—in India's case it is DRDO—in order to design new weapons, equipment and special infrastructure for the Armed Forces.

In drawing up the defence policy and war plans of a state in support of the political policy of the state, the strategians have to consider the types of war, size, shape, climate, composition of the Armed Forces, technological, economic development and war potential of the country.

7.5 Lesson To Be Learnt

Basically, a Military Geography functions as a part of education for both survival and triumph:

1. Policy-Decision-makers must review national characteristics, resources and its condition, aim and objectives before launching military operation.
2. Specific battlefield conditions—Geographical affect—not only the tactics to be employed but the weapons and equipments which will be required.
3. Military Geography affects socio-economic environment condition and civil-military relations.
4. Military Geography is forced to maintain the proportion between Geographical extensions of the battlefield and war potential of the country. Imbalance may be one of the causes for defeat. During World War II, the Germans were unable to hold the conquered territory of Soviet Russia, owing to inequilibrium between the strength of German Army and extension of the battlefield in Soviet Russia.[8]
5. Political aim of war can be achieved through military means: "Military power is one of the instruments. If it is

decided to be used, then study of Military Geography is vital." Though the advanced science and technology has minimised the importance of Military Geography, it still holds its position as a significant factor in the process of war planning and programming. Military Geography is expanded in a wider context and has become an academic discipline, applying geography to the conduct of war including matters unique to land, naval and air warfare. Modern development of the concepts of warfare and the expansion of the area of military interest and responsibility has forced an expansion of Military Geography and hence it is to be recognised as an 'Academic Discipline'.

Footnotes

1. A.P. Choudhary, *Military Geography,* Nirali Prakashan, Pune, 1995, pp. 5-6.
2. Louis C. Peltier and G.Etzel Pearcy, *Military Geography,* Affiliated East West Press, Pvt. Ltd. 92 Montieth Road, Chennai-8, India 1981, p.15.
3. *Ibid.*, p.7.
4. Bikash B. Basu, "Role of Air Power In Military Geography," *USI Journal,* July- Sept 1994, Kashmir House, King Georges Avenue, New Delhi-11, p.40.
5. "Precis on Military Geography", by Geography Dept N.D.A. Khadakwasla, Pune, 1999, p.4.
6. Louis C. Peltier and G. Etzel Pearcy, *op. cit.,* p. 18-19.
7. Winston S. Churchill, *The Second World War,* Educational Book Company Ltd., 1950, London, UK. pp. 29-32.
8. Louis C. Peltier and G. Etzel Pearcy, *op. cit.,* p. 16-17.

8

GRAND STRATEGY, STRATEGY AND TACTICS

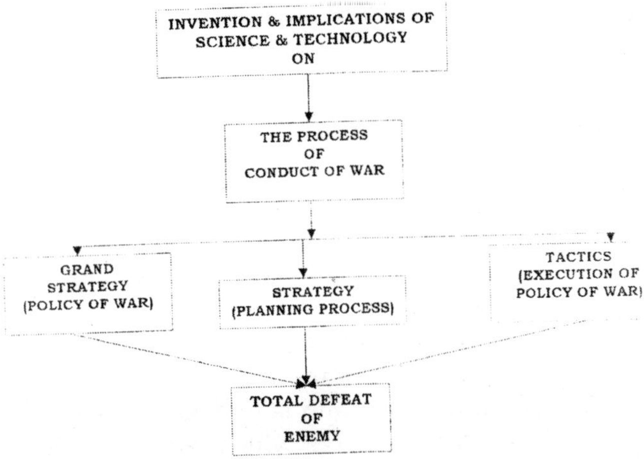

8.1 INTRODUCTION

It was the "Industrial Revolution" which introduced the evolutionary and revolutionary changes in civil and military sectors. Industrialisation had introduced the drastic changes in society. On the eve of Industrialisation and its implication, the nature of war became more complex. The invention in Science and Technology had brought the revolutionary changes in overall process of the cònduct of war.[1] "War" became an essential but complicated affair of the "State" which had reflected in emergence of General Staff and rise of professional standing army. In Europe, it was the Gustavas Adolphus, the then king of Sweden who had visualised the scope and significance of war and introduced at first the "Permanent standing Army". So war became more offensive, mobile, costly and destructive in every respect. And it was necessary to conduct war with certain aim, policy, planning, and preparation. So to conduct a war with certain preparation, aim, policy, planning and its execution it introduced the process of war i.e. Grand Strategy, Strategy and Tactics.

Grand Strategy, Strategy, and Tactics—these three different terminologies are used synonymously but logically they have different meaning, scope and purview though having interlinkages. Therefore, it is highly essential to deal and clear every concept independently.

8.1 Grand Strategy

8.1.1 Meaning and Concept

The word Grand "itself indicates that it has a wider meaning and scope". Grand Strategy means a national policy and every country has a national policy but the nature of policy during war and peace would be different. Every country during "Peace" has (aim) policy to maintain her freedom at every cost. But during war it should be to defeat an enemy by every possible means and maintain its freedom and sovereignty. So the basic aim is to defeat the enemy by all possible means and resources which the country has to mobilise and utilise to conduct the war.

In view of the above facts it can be concluded that every nation has a Grand Strategy. National Grand Strategy means "it's art and science of developing and using the political, economic and psychological powers of a nation together, with its armed forces during peace and war". The Grand Strategy may be defined as a process of planning for coordination and direction of all resources of a country in order to attain and retain a political objective". Grand Strategy means a policy which guides how to conduct the war. [2] In other words, it is an act to develop the economic resources and manpower of a nation in order to sustain the combat forces.

8.1.2 Formation of Grand Strategy

It's a policy of the war, which can be decided unanimously. It is the Government who decides to take initiative to determine the Grand Strategy. The leaders and eminent persons from various fields and sectors were supposed to be invited including Chiefs and Deputy Chiefs of the various services i.e. Army, Navy Airforce etc. After discussion whatever conclusion is drawn is called Grand Strategy. The Government needs the support from every sector of the (society) country to conduct the war. Therefore eminent persons, leaders from various fields like Industry, Economic, Religion are invited in the process of formulation of Grand Strategy. For example, in the seventies the west Pakistani forces intervened on East Pakistan and started harassment of the innocent and unarmed people. To get rid of this the citizens of East Pakistan immigrated and took shelter in India. Such immigration created tremendous pressure on Indian economy. And country like India, a developing country, how long can she afford this burden unnecessarily due to anarchy in East Pakistan by the armed forces of West Pakistan. So in view of this problem **India's Grand Strategy during 1971 war was to create the peaceful situation in East Pakistan.** [3] It meant to thrash out the West Pakistan forces from East Pakistan who were doing a lot of injustice to the peoples of East Pakistan. So this was the Grand Strategy of India.

8.1.3 Commitment of Grand Strategy

Grand Strategy does not mean only plan, direct or coordinate and control over the resources but it is practically "Grand". It does not suppose to meet only present situation or requirement but it has to provide a future. Grand Strategy deals with post war problems. It must be capable of having a vision and action for the future. In this connection Liddell Hart rightly said:

"Grand Strategy looks beyond the war to the subsequent peace.[4]"

It means that Grand Strategy must provide ways and means to solve the problems which will be the part of post war situation. This might be the reason that India played a very crucial role after 1971 war in the "Process of Building" East Pakistan as an Independent state— Bangladesh. It was the United States of America who dropped Nuclear Bomb over Japanese cities of Nagasaki and Hiroshima and brought the World War II to an end. But to meet the post war situation and sort out the problems through Truman and Marshall Plan, America spent huge amount of money to restore the situation in Japan. Even during World War II though the conflict continued between Allied Forces and Axis but the planning to tackle the post war situation was already chalked out. The famous "Atlantic Charter" became the foundation of United Nations. This UN Charter was discussed and tentatively prepared during World War II only.

Grand Strategy must be formed with care and foresight. Grand Strategy means high level selection of object is made by scientific appreciation of the various important factors as:

a) Military strength of enemy

b) Scientific research and development

c) Economy and war potential

Political aspect is also to be considered according to pre war conditions. It was then that India had signed a treaty of friendship with the U.S.S.R before the 1971 war. The reason was that U.S.A. and China had assured to assist Pakistan and deter India from interfering in actual conflict on behalf of Pakistan, if the situation required. In view of this possible threat India then signed a treaty of friendship with the U.S.S.R and ensured that if China or America would interfere, the U.S.S.R could definitely assist India at this crucial juncture.[5]

8.1.4 Tools of Grand Strategy

The basic aim of Grand Strategy is to develop and employ the economic resources and man-power of a country to keep a nation in a perfect state of defence preparedness. The Government must proceed for war accordingly. Military power is one of the tools of Grand Strategy and it is to be used as a last resort. Grand Strategians must apply the various tools like indirect pressure, negotiation, commercial pressure, economic warfare, unfriendly act, diplomatic pressure against enemy. When all methods will fail to yield the expected result, only then the last option i.e. use of force is supposed to be preferred. Basically, there were three major steps to use the tools of strategy.

i) **Pursuit For Peaceful Settlement:** Now-a-days "Crunch of Resources" is a common problem of third world countries and even super powers also have a number of problems. In view of these "problems", an attempt should be made to sort out the issue by peaceful means, like dialogue with concerned country, mediation by neutral state or common friend of both countries and even conciliation would be one of the options. All this depends on which peaceful effort can produce the result. In some cases commission of inquiry or International Tribunal was also constituted, which had given the Judgement. During 1965 Pakistan had declared "Rann of Kutch" as a disputed territory as a result of it; International Tribunal, was constituted to decide the facts. According to judgement given by International Tribunal, India surrendered some portion of the Rann of Kutch to Pakistan.

ii) **Hostile Acts:** This is the second stage of the "Grand Strategy" in which numbers of hostile activities can be carried out. This includes indirect conflict at socio-cultural, psychological, economic and political front at domestic, regional and global level against an enemy i.e. hostile state. Psychological warfare is meant to gear-up the resources to create critical attitude of the masses against the hostile state at domestic, regional and global levels. Another tool is socio-cultural and religious disparities. On the basis of such disparities the tension can mount up within enemy's territory. In this stage an attempt has to be made at every level. Also on the economic front steps against the enemy would be taken and his economic interest could be jeopardised. There were a number of stages of economic warfare, economic sanctions, denial of trade capital, resources, and blockade against the hostile state. Even industrial strike, can also be managed in the enemy's state in order to cripple his war potential and economic sources. The tools of economic warfare must be executed in an effective manner.

iii) **War:** When the above measures fail to yield an acceptable or expected solution, then the last resort remains before using Grand Strategy is the use of force. In this third stage other unfriendly acts like blockade at a specific points, aggressive condemnation at every level whenever and whatever it is possible, deployment of troops with all preparations and opening a major furry against enemy. The basic aim of war is to impose the will upon hostile state by use of force and not only to carry out devastation and destruction in enemy territory. [6]

8.2 STRATEGY — Process of Planning

Strategy "means preparation for war" in every respect to wage a war. The changing nature of war, threat perceptions and Revolution in Military Affairs had introduced the drastic changes in *modus operandi,* of war. In view of these changes, conduct of war without planning and foresight, calculations is just impossible. The term strategy is accomplished with every aspect of planning of war. Strategy is derived indirectly from Greek word **Stratego and Strategma** meaning tricks of war. It is an art and even science to control the forces. It is the art of a military commander to project and direct a campaign or handle the forces during war. Its process unites means with ends.

"Strategy" word has a wider meaning and aspect, it requires the consideration of non-military factors like socio-cultural economic, political, psychological, and hence it became an inherent element of statecraft during peace too. So strategy can be used during war and even peace to attend the intended goal in any sector.

8.2.3 National Strategy During Peace and War

In view of a wider context of strategy, it is apparent that every nation has a strategy during war and peace. It is vital to focus a strategy during war and peace.

a) During Peace:

1. Maintain the freedom, sovereignty and independence of the country.
2. Protect the boundaries with vigilance.
3. Without any use of force national interests should be protected.
4. Obtain information about enemy in every respect.
5. Carry out the modernisation programme for the armed forces.
6. Have or arrange an alliance with super powers or a country more potential than that of one's own.
7. Improve the capability which could affect enemy and even international politics, community.
8. Dominate the enemy in economic, political and socio-cultural fields.
9. While carrying out an effort for overall development of the country, adequate attention should be paid to improve the living standard of the peoples.
10. Attend the spectacular progress of the country in every field and emphasize on invention and research in science and technology.
11. Development of the country should be concentrated on industrial basis because industrial development is an access to attend the economic, military and socio-cultural development.

12. Attempts should be made to carry out the unrest and confusion in politics and industrial sector of hostile state. Even attempt should be made to mount up the communal tension in enemy's state.

b. **During War:**

1 Utilise, mobilise, coordinate and control the resources for the conduct of war. Top priority should be given to defence preparedness of the country and wastage or misuse of resources must be avoided.

2. All the resources of the country, once the planning and mobilisation is over, must be used with economy and foresight.
3. Compel the enemy to accept the condition which we expected.
4. An attempt should be made to achieve the aim of war without hard fighting.
5. Push vigorously your enemy into a critical condition or create miserable condition for the enemy.
6. In order to cripple down the enemies' war potential, it is a must for the country to adopt various measures of economic warfare and carry out strategic bombing at transportation, communication, installations, oil fields, coal mines, gas deposits etc. The enemy should realise that he cannot afford a war.
7. Mount-up the types of pressure upon allied states of our enemy and to ensure that they neither would actually interfere nor will support directly or indirectly during war period.
8. Maintain the unity, integrity, coordination and cooperation within the various ministries, organisations, committees, non-governmental organisations including Central and State Governments etc to attend the aim, policy and objective of war.
9. It's the art and duty of operational commander to maintain the enthusiasm, coordination, cooperation

within the various combat branches on the actual ground.

10. Government has to mobilise all the required resources in a manner that there is no break-up or interruption in logistics supply under any circumstances. Logistics is the key factor to conduct and wage the war successfully.
11. Especially the religious leaders should put all efforts to maintain the socio-cultural cohesiveness within the various communities and support the Government.
12. To have more access, rights, liberty to conduct and wage a war successfully, Government may declare the "Emergency". [8]

8.2.4 Definitions

Once the "Grand Strategy" is determined, the job of top military leaders begins, no political leaders are supposed to interfere in this process of a strategy. "Strategy" is a purview of top level military officers and hence no space is left for any interference by politicians or beurocrats. Now the task to attend the aim of war is handed over to the Military Generals by the politicians. The Government is bound to procure the requirements of the combat forces and make available all the required resources. In the light of this distribution of assignment, the politicians have to concentrate on domestic front and conduct of external relations in addition to the mobilising, coordinating, directing and controlling the resources. They are supposed to review the situation, position, available means and resources in order to attain the aim of war policy. According to the definition of Liddell Hart, "Strategy is the art of military leaders to distribute and apply the military means to fulfill the aim of policy." In a nutshell, strategy means the theory of the use of combat forces to attain the policy of war. Clausewits, the well-known military thinker, defines strategy as the "art of the employment of battles as a means to gain the object of war". In accordance with this definition it is to be understood that it's the Military Generals who will decide that how the available forces, firepower, will be displayed according to threat, perceptions, priorities and strategic importance. Whereas the Cyril Falls explained the strategy as a means of moving or disposition of troops with the object of dictating to the enemy the place, time and nature of the battle. [9]

In view of the definitions given by these scholars for proper understanding of "strategy", India's example in this regard can be pointed out. During 1971 i.e. Bangladesh Freedom Movement, India had to fight a war against Pakistan on the two fronts, Western Front where India shares her land border with Pakistan and on the "Eastern Front" which was very crucial in relation to the basic aim of war. Taking into consideration the significance and scope of the eastern front, Military Generals of India adopted offensive posture on the eastern front and concentrated their maximum potential. It was vital because in relation to the aim of war the eastern front was a "decisive" front. On the western front India adopted defensive posture and detained minimum and essential forces just to defend the boundary. On account of excellent strategy adopted by Indian Military Generals they had attended spectacular victory against Pakistan in 1971 war. Such victory was possible due to accuracy in calculation and coordination of the means and resources given to them and its systematic use.

8.2.3 Aim and Action of Strategy

The meaning and even some of the definitions highlight the basic aim of strategy i.e. to achieve the goal of policy. Though the basic aim of the strategy is to attain the goal of policy but it cannot be attained unless and until the effective result-oriented use of force is employed. And use of force does not mean the destruction of enemy, if the goal of war policy is fulfilled by placing him in a critical condition. It is not necessary to carry out destruction and devastation of the enemy. The aim of strategy is to disrupt, dislocate and distract enemy so that his resistance paralyse him and will not be in a position to fight against you.

To attain the aim of strategy, the action of strategy would be "Deception and Dislocation" both physically and psychologically. The Deception of enemy is the soul of every operation which has relevance to well-known principles of war i.e. secrecy and surprise. If you want your strategy to be successful then you must dupe your enemy. If you could give a jerk of surprise to your enemy, he will not be able to reinforce, regroup, redeploy his forces. Deception is the base for physical and psychological dislocation of the enemy. Dislocation of the enemy both physically and psychologically depends on the quality of weapons, element of secrecy and surprise. If the enemy is in a large number and size, he can be dislocated and scattered by the use of heavy fire power.[10] The enemy's force will be physically dislocated. The psychological dislocation is more relevant to boldness, courage and moral of the enemy. In the action of strategy "psychological dislocation is more relevant to psychological warfare rather than defence preparedness". There are a number of examples which can be quoted in this context. During the seventeenth century, Shivaji had launched a raid on Shahista Khan at Red Mahal of Pune. This was an unexpected raid by Shivaji in early dawn which caught the Mughal camp in a great surprise and confusion. This had psychological result—Shahista Khan was demoralised and he found very uneasy calm in the red palace of Pune. And at last he left Pune and arrived at Aurangabad. [11] This is an example of psychological dislocation of enemy.

During World War II, the British forces were prepared to face any attack from the sea in Malaya. But Japanese forces by crossing the dense forest of Siam border, attacked from land. British forces were in a great confusion and found absolutely unprepared to meet such attack from land border. [12]

8.3 TACTICS

The strategy and tactics, these two different words are generally used synonymously though they are linked with each other and have relevance to the conduct of war. Strategy is the art of projecting and directing a campaign whereas the tactics is the art of handling the forces in the battle. Strategy lies mainly in the sphere of communication; tactics is in the domain of field Commanders. Strategy is determined by top level military officers whereas tactics has to be determined at the bottom level, according to changes and possibility, feasibility on the actual ground, by the local field commander.

Tactics is the art and even the science of fighting the battle. Tactics means an execution of strategy by actual use of force. It's a skill of local military leader to employ the available manpower, weapons, and equipments in order to achieve the strategy. Clausewits, the well known scholar, defines tactics as a "theory of using Military Forces in battle". Actually tactics is an art based on the knowledge of how to make "men to fight with their maximum energy against an enemy." Liddell Hart also defined tactics, in a simple manner: 'Tactics is an art of field commander in the deployment of his men and employment of weapons in the actual battlefield with a view to achieve the aim of strategy.'

The success of tactics depends upon the local field commander, it may happen that his counterpart i.e. enemy may be superior in terms of number of soldiers and weapons. Now it depends on how he will conduct and manoeuvre on the actual ground, how he will employ the means and weapons effectively against his enemy. History of warfare is a witness for it, that despite critical condition the Military commander introduced the new tactics, method of fighting, skill and defeated their enemy.[13] For example, during 1947-48 Indo-Pak war, it was Gen. Thimayya who had climbed-up the tanks at Jozila pass and compelled the Pakistani soldiers to flee from Jozila pass. This Jozila pass, was strategically and even tactically too important, without it the further conduct of war could not have been possible for the Indian Forces.[14] Another instant of Maratha art of warfare, the founder of Hindvi Swarajya and King Chhatrapati Shivaji who had introduced the guerrilla tactics against the Mughals, Adilshahs, Nizam etc. As compared to his enemy Shivaji had very poor resources but due to "Guerrilla tactics" he had not only sustained against powerful enemies but from time to time, defeated them many times.

Success of tactics depends on the following factors:

- Observation, raid, ambush, fire power
- Strength of soldiers and their standard of training
- Patrol, intelligence, sophisticated W and E
- Morale and leadership
- Camouflage and concealment
- Tactical manoeuverability
- Study of local geography and circumstances
- Enemy's position based on material facts
- Command, control and communication

It is apparent that the aim of tactics is very limited and confined with battlefield and actual facts of the situation, time available and resources of both the entity.

Footnotes

1. Edward M. Earle, Editor, *Makers of Modern Strategy,* Natraj Publisher, Dehradun, 2003, pp. 9-11.
2. Louis C. Peltier and G Etzel Pearcy, *Military Geography,* Affiliated East West Press, 92, Montieth Road, Chennai, 1981, pp. 31-32.
3. Precis on *Grand Strategy, Strategy and Tactics,* Department of Defence and Strategic Studies, University of Pune., Pune-7, 1982.
4. Major Jodh Singh, *War: Its Principles, Tactics and Strategies,* Surjeet Publication, Kolhapur Road, Kamla Nagar, Delhi-7 1980) p. 72.
5. Precis on *Grand Strategy, Strategy and Tactics, op.cit.,* DDSS, Pune, 1982
6. Louis C. Peltier and G. Etzel Pearcy, *op. cit.,* pp. 32-33

7. Edward M. Earle, *op. cit.*, p. 8
8. Precis on *Grand Strategy, Strategy and Tactics, op. cit.*,
9. Major Jodh Singh, *op. cit.*, p. 73.
10. Precis on *Grand Strategy, Strategy and Tactics, op. cit.*
11. Sarkar J.N., *Shivaji and His Times*, Orient Longman Publisher, New Delhi, 1966, pp. 35-37.
12. M.G.Abhyankar (Lt.Col.), *Defence Principles and Organisation*, Usha Prakashan, University of Pune, Pune-7, 1974, p.83.
13. Major Jodh Singh, *op. cit.*, p. 74-75.
14. M.G. Abhyankar, *op. cit.*, p. 79-80.
15. Brig. K.G. Pitre, *War History of Marathas, 1600-1848*, Books and Books Company, New Delhi, 1996, pp. 86-88.
16. Major Jodh Singh, *op. cit.*, p. 74-76.

✤ ✤ ✤

9

ROLE OF GEOGRAPHY IN LAND, SEA AND AIR WARFARE

9.1 INTRODUCTION

There is not an iota of doubt that War and Geography have certain co-relationship. Every war is influenced by the geography of a battlefield. And hence it becomes vital to study the specific geographical features that affect the process of the conduct of war i.e. from Grand Strategy to Tactics. It is geography that forced the Governments and its executive agents to consider all geographical factors—from weather to size—for the successful conduct of war. Whatever type of the warfare it may be—either it is sea, air or land warfare—"Mobility and Accessibility" is going to be affected by geographical factors. An attempt is made to evaluate the role of Geography in Air, Sea and Land warfare.

9.1 Role of Geography in Land Warfare:

9.1.1 Meaning and Concept

Land warfare means its direct imposition of force upon people through destruction or control of the means and through occupation and exercise of political control. During land warfare two things are to be remembered:

1. We must visualise the limits to military capabilities.

2. And secondly we must be aware of the "time frame of military operation".

In land warfare it is assumed that destruction or control of the enemies—"Armed Force, munition industry and commercial activity complex"—will take place. In view of the meaning of land warfare it can be defined as "its capability of fighting, occupation of commercial, industrial and political centers and the imposition of political rule through occupation or puppet regime.[1] The history of Afghanistan is a distinct example in this regard. At present the America's policy towards Iraq and Afghanistan is to be understood in this context. Needless to say, that the Government of Afghanistan led by Dr. Hamid Karzai is a puppet of U.S.A.

The geography of land warfare is centric with military objective and their accessibility—while it revolves around the Regional Geometry and Military objectives. The local geography includes channels, obstacles and its effects by weather and seasonal changes. In land warfare the accessibility—vulnerability is the most important aspect. As far as accessibility is concerned, it includes the choice of means of movement, routes, time, distance, net traffic, load capacity, use of local condition and the most crucial factor i.e. vulnerability of routes.

Local Geography affects the capacity of armed forces, use of local conditions, camouflage and concealment, freedom to manoeuvre, range of contact with enemy, availability of local supplies, and transportation facilities, potentiality of ambushing and the role of local population. [2] Location of the target is one of the important aspects—it is the location of target which will decide the time, nature of action and accessibility. Whereas size of the area of operation will decide the strength of the land forces with nature of action and use of fire power. And the nature of terrain will decide the type of land warfare; either it will be jungle, plain, desert or high altitude warfare.

9.1.2 Factors Affecting Land Warfare:

1. **Space Dimension:** Space and time are more important regarding the existent matter. It is land geography which will decide the nature of tactics in an actual combat operation.
2. **Terrain of the land:** Terrain has the implications of mobility and movement. If the terrain is plain and flat, then accordingly means of transportation will have to be made available. Nonetheless to mention that in plain area train, vehicles, aircrafts can be employed on a large scale. So the nature of terrain will decide the course of action and the problem of accessibility.
3. **Material of the area:** The nature of land will decide the nature of the vehicle. Either it is rock, hard or smooth soil? Hard strata will provoke to employ the TANKS and APC on a large scale. And desert area has no choice rather than camels. So it is the nature of the land which will decide the nature of the vehicles—APC, Tanks and Aircrafts etc.—to be employed. [3]
4. **Drainage Pattern:** Drainage are more protective to move towards the location of the target during combat operation. It is one of the options to hide from enemies' sight. Moving towards target via drainage is most useful as it provides "secrecy" and security from direct observation by the enemy. Drainage can be an obstacle in terms of mobility and fire power.
5. **Other Obstacles:** As far as obstacles are concerned, there are two types of obstacles, i.e. Natural and Man-made.

   During land warfare forest, rivers, mountains can be obstacles and even man-made obstacles can be hazardous i.e. canals, settlement of colonies, mines, ditches, trenches etc.

6. **Climate and Weather:** "Climate" reflects the long term perspective whereas weather reflects variation and changes for a certain period. Local weather can affect the movements of land forces. Suddenly rain and fog will hamper the mobility and visibility of the ground forces.[4] It can be considered that size and character of the army and its organisation are determined by the geographical features of a political area.

9.2 Role of Geography in Sea Warfare

9.2.1 Meaning and Concept:

"If you protect the maritime boundaries then only you would successfully protect the land boundaries. And whoever had negligence towards "Sea Protection" had a subject of Mercy by other."

—Said A.T. Mahan—the great exponent of the importance of sea power. The history of warfare is a witness to it. In modern age, conducting a war in sea, high seas, is a tremendously complicated and expensive task. Naval forces have to fight with the enemy in deep ocean and simultaneously negotiate with geographical factors which affect in a negative manner. Victory in sea-warfare mainly consisted of "Accessibility and Mobility". Accessibility means a capacity to apply the "power" towards the target and mobility means ability to move from one place to another which can more efficiently approach a target to cover a maximum distance in a stipulated time. It is highly essential because the speed of advance and radius of action have been the most important considerations in "Naval Strategy".[5]

9.2.2 Geographical Factors Affecting Conduct of Sea Warfare

1) **Nature of Sea Coast:** The nature of sea coast is the gift given by nature. It is the nature of sea coast which will affect the 'mobility'. We can see that the structure of sea coast is different from place to place—somewhere it will be man-made coast or ports and in some cases it's natural.

2) **Transport:** Transportation is one of the determinant factors in order to reach the desired destination. But in some ocean—in deep sea—we can find snow, rock, vegetation, and this can affect the mobility negatively. In some deep sea you cannot find any sort of obstacles; on the contrary, you would attain more mobility.

3) **Distance:** Distance "between starting point and target will decide the time". Short distance is one of the determinant factors to reach the desired place in order to attain victory. If you could reach the desired place much before than your enemy could, then you will be able to dictate the terms and dominate the enemy as well as the battle.[6] And it is possible when the distance is short, for example—"Lakshadweep Island"—before Pakistani arrived there, Indian navy had reached over there and hoisted the Indian Flag. Actually Pakistan was under wrong estimate when her Naval ship moved towards the Lakshadweep Island but when they approached very close to Lakshadweep they realised that "it's of no use at all" because Indian Forces already had occupied the position. This was an episode of post partition era of India-Pakistan. U.S. Naval communication network has been spread up throughout the world. And especially distance between their Homeland and Afro-Asian countries was more than desirable. In order to minimise the negative effect of "long distance", Americans have established the communication centre at Diego Garcia Island with the aim to fill up the gap of worldwide communication network of U.S.A.

4) **Weather Condition:** The weather condition has close relevance to near or remote places. The state of sea exerts a strong influence on tactical movements. Like high waves reduce the speed of ships and disturb steering system, the veil of rains affect the range of visibility. Winds or gales can

disperse or destroy the ships and aircrafts. Manoeuverability becomes difficult by such hazards. Winds more than 115 miles per hour tend to impair the safety of parachute landing. Survival in a gale is very difficult.

5) **Water Current:** In depth of sea, water current is also one of the hazards. Its scientific as well as natural phenomenon is a sort of water circulation. In deep sea, warm water raises over the sea face and cold water goes down. So the warm-cold water going up and coming down generates currents. Such water current proves as one of the hazards for smooth movements of the ships.

6) **Clouds:** Clouds can be hazardous while conducting sea warfare, smoothly. Basically the clouds limit the "observation" process. The clouds pose a threat in a negative manner to the process of observation. [7]

7) **Straits:** Straits are considered a subject of strategic importance. It has come up as a means of controlling shipping and confining navies. The history of naval warfare is a witness for it. For example, battles of Trafalgar in A.D.1805; Jutland in A.D. 1916; and Tsushima in 1905, all these battles took place in straits. This supports the fact that straits are the subjects of strategic importance in sea-warfare.

8) **Port Facilities:** Geography of a port has certain amount of capacity. It has some limitations about landing. Landing facilities are related to transport facilities. Geography of ports must provide better efficiency and facilities. An amount of transport and escort function of Naval force, ports and landing beaches also stand out as pertinent to the science of sea-warfare. The geography of ports, harbours, coasts has relevance to loading and unloading, repair and logistics supply facilities. So, geography of a port decidedly control the facilities including their nature and limitation. [8]

Now-a-days in sea warfare maximum concentration is being given on "sea routes and shipping lanes". Very forcefully the concept of "Lifeline" came up, in which sea lanes-routes have a strategic significance. Lifeline is a junction between homeland and its nearby area (colonies). During World War II, the British had a "lifeline"—sea route—through Mediterranean Sea.

9.3 Role of Geography in Air Warfare

9.3.1 Meaning and Concept

The Wright Brothers of America invented an aircraft. During World War I an idea of employment of the aircraft for combat purpose was criticised. But despite such criticism, Germany had employed the air craft on a large scale during World War I. During World War II, exclusively, the Air power played expected role. It was the American Air Force and British Royal Air Force who had carried out a "Strategic Bombing" with deep penetration into Germany. In view of the role of air power during Second World War and its positive result, the air power has become an essential and integral part of the Armed Forces of the respective countries. And even from World War II onwards, whatever conflict took place, the "Air Power" proved its ability and significance as the decisive war winning factor.[9]

a) **Airspace:** According to Paris Convention of 1919: "A Nation has complete sovereignty over the air space above its territorial frontiers and waters." It means any aircraft entering the airspace of another country without any prior permission will be treated as violation of sovereignty of airspace and the Nation has right to take suitable military action against the invader.

b) **Air Power:** At the initial stage air power was defined as the total ability of a nation to fly, to act through the air space and to use, controlled flight for the purpose of war. Thus it is the absolute authority of a nation to assert its military will via the medium of the air. In the modern context air power being defined that its ability of a nation to deploy its aircrafts and weaponary in the strategic, tactical and logistics role to achieve the maximum advantages of mobility and firepower offered by airspace.

9.3.2 Role of Air Power In Modern Warfare

In view of the "role of the Air Power" during World War II and successfull results in post World War II era have generated the hopes and aspiration for air power. The following factors are to be considered while identifying the role of air power:-

- Identification of target and task
- Accessibility from the base.

"Air Warfare" is a warfare which can be fought over the land and also on sea. The fate and results of battles can be determined by the successful and systematic use of air power. The history of post World War II era is a witness to it. The expected role of air power is as follows:

9.3.3 Functional Aspects:

a) **Strategic Role:** To carry out the bombing at the strategic point will have certain implications to conduct a war for the enemy. It can be termed as a long term result-oriented action. For example, the strategic bombing which was carried out by UK and USA during Second World War against Germany crippled the war potential. And to defend over airspace from enemy's aggression and deny the same to the enemy.

b) **Tactical Role:** It includes launching a raid and carrying out destruction and devastation in enemy's territory. To conduct the patrol; reconnaissance and surveillance, tactical function also incorporates i.e. to provide escort and close support to the ground forces.

c) **Logistics Role:** Basically it provides "transport services" with extreme mobility. To carry out the injured soldiers for medical relief, and to deliver goods and commodities including ammunition required by the combat soldiers are two more functions. [10]

In view of the increasing and exclusive role of air power, planning and training are important aspects. To conduct such mission involves specific consideration of geographical factors like weather, terrain, location and size etc. Geographical factors affect numbers of functions of air power—flight conditions, contact to Navigation efficiency of reconnaissance etc. Though research and modification to improve the potential of air power are continuing but the geographical factor still holds its importance in affecting air warfare.

9.4 The Geographical Factors affecting Air Warfare are as follows:

1) **Location:** To perform positive result-oriented role, the locations of a target (concerned state) both physical and regarding vicinity plays a crucial role. It is the location of targets where it is located. The combat mission should be able to reach their target by the shortest route without the necessity of overflying the air space of neighboring state. And such overflying requires political permission.

2) **Size:** The size of the country determines the airspace. The military evaluation of size is based on the fundamental principle of maintaining an effective ratio between the strength of air force and available air space. The vast air space offers advantages to have a large commercial and powerful military components of air power. Flexibility in planning, the strategic, tactical and logistical operational plan for defensive and offensive action have to be prepared carefully if the country possesses "large air space". A country like India enjoys a large airspace but the ratio between "space and force" is not satisfactory in order to move it effectively for defensive and offensive roles.

3) **Terrain:** An element of terrain also could affect the expected role of air power. Mountainous terrain or

high altitude poses problems for tactical as well as logistics role. For example, the low density of air over certain region reduces the load-carrying capacity of aircrafts. In some of the terrain choppers, Helicopters cannot be deployed for offering battlefield mobility. The mountainous regions pose difficulty for tactical fire and another disadvantage is that lack of feasible landing arrangement limits the operational process.

4) **Weather and Climate:** Despite an advancement in the field of "aviation" weather still holds a position of an "hazard" in the process of deployment of aircraft and guided weapons. It is a handicap in order to establish command of the air. Weather condition affects operational base area as well as target area. Moreover, weather affects operational efficiency of air warfare. During pre and post monsoon and also during thunder storms, flying activities are seriously affected due to turbulent weather conditions. Fog reduces surface visibility to less than 1000 meters. Even fire power can be affected by temperature in various ways.

5) **Wind:** "Wind" is one of the geographical components which could affect air operation in a negative manner. "Wind" affects the speed and courses of a projectile and the bombing capability of aircrafts. In mountainous region the local wind conditions may prevent air entirely. Wind is an ideal means of dispersing fog but over 80 kilometer per hour it can disperse concentration of ships and aircrafts.[11]

6) **Clouds and Fog:** Clouds and fog also limit the ability to observe and engage the enemy and they can mask the advantages of moonlight or sky glow at night. In some areas early cloud showers or fog can obscure images or sights. Mountains or hill tops making low-level air operations are quite hazardous. And both cloud and fog can limit the range of radio communications.

Radar technology and the electronic guidance system have removed certain limitations on operational efficiency imposed by weather like lowering of visibility due to fog, clouds and atmospheric imparities.

Over and above the following geographical factors also affect air warfare:

1. Prevailing weather condition
2. Relations to the "Air Bases"
3. Accessibility and its efficiency
4. Relative distribution of friendly and enemical installation etc.[12]

Footnotes

1. Louis C. Peltier and G. Etzel Pearcy, *Military Geography,* East West Pvt. Ltd., Montieth Road, Chennai 8. 1966, p.52.
2. *Ibid.*, p.54.
3. M.G. Abhyankar, Lt. Col., *Defence Principles and Organisation,* Usha Prakashan, Pune University, Pune 7, 1974 p.140.
4. Precis on *Military Geography,* Department of Defence and Strategic Studies, University of Pune, Ganeshkhind, Pune 7. 1982.
5. Louis C. Peltier and G. Etzel Pearcy, *op. cit.,* p.55.
6. M.G. Abhyankar, Lt.Col., *op. cit.,* p.84.
7. *Cadet's Hand Book,* N.C.C. Naval Wing, Published by Mah. Naval Unit, NCC Mumbai, 2005, pp. 171-72.
8. Louis C. Peltier and G. Etzel Pearcy, *op. cit.,* p.57.
9. Bikash B. Basu, Role of Air Power in Military Geography, *USI Journal,* July-Sep 1991, Kashmir House, King George Avenues, New Delhi, pp. 41-42.
10. Major Jodh Singh, Retd, *War: Its Principles, Tactics and Strategies,* Surjeet Publication, 7K, Kolhapur Road, Kamla Nagar, Delhi, 1980, pp. 61-62.

11. Interview/Discussion, Lt. Dr. P. A. Ghosh, Naval/Wing, N.C.C. officer on 28/7/06 Deptt. of Defence and Strategic Studies, Bhonsala Military College, Nasik 5, M.S.

12. M.A. Harvey, Major, "Weather As A Factor In Tactical Planning", *Army Journal,* Vol. 5, No-56, 1991, The Russian Press Pvt. Ltd, Moscow, pp. 10-11.

✣ ✣ ✣

10

AN UNDERSTANDING OF LOGISTICS MANAGEMENT

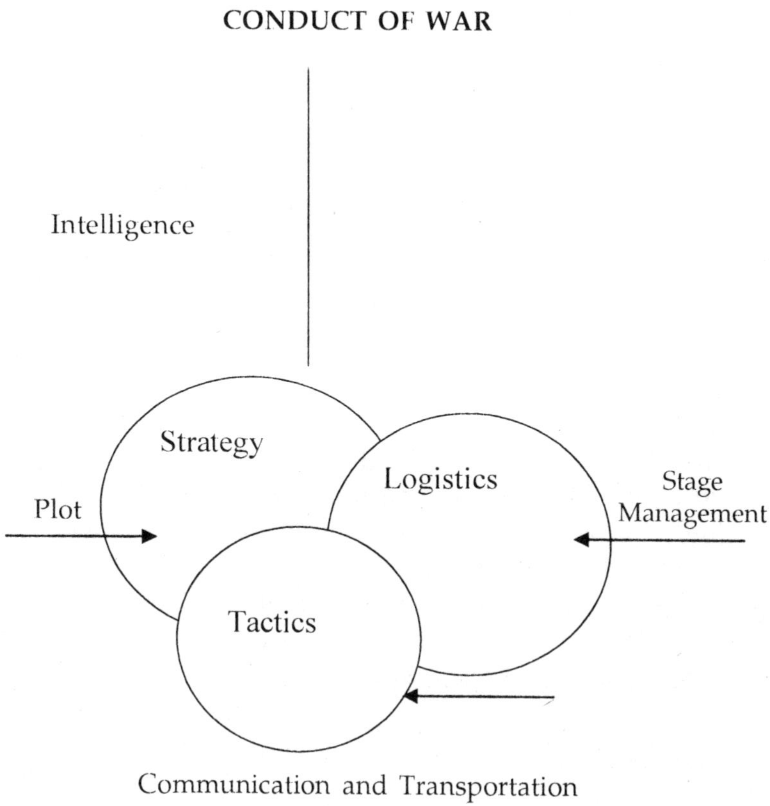

10. INTRODUCTION

Logistics is an Organisation which is mainly responsible to procure the requirement of the combat forces. When this Organisation meets the requirements of the forces systematically and in a satisfied manner, then it becomes a logistic management. It's the responsibility of logistic management to ensure that every soldier, vehicle, while pushing off towards the battlefield is well prepared in a perfect manner. This management has to provide all the "services" relevant to conduct of war i.e. medical, workshop, food, water, ammunition etc. The role of logistics management is a wider and crucial one during war as well as peace. During war this logistic services are termed as a "war administration".

Logistics management is a part of non-combat services.

10.1 Definitions

1. Logistics is a military application of the process of "getting the most for your money" and maintaining the highest level of efficiency.
2. The American approach: "It's a science of planning to carry out the movements and maintenance of forces."[1] It is a fact that logistics is the science which is concerned with actual support to the combat forces and normally expected maximum benefits by spending minimum cost.
3. Brig. G.S. Kohali explains: "Logistic supply is an old phenomenon; it is being recognised after industrial revolution. Logistics means importing the raw material and distribute the goods and commodities." [2] According to Indian view logistics means a supply of essential and useful goods and commodities to the combat soldiers in order to achieve the aim of war.
4. Logistics is the process of starting the tactics to achieve the "strategy".

10.2 Meaning and Concept

Logistics means a supply of required goods and commodities to the combat forces specially during war, and even in peace too. Logistics in other words is a "war potential" of the country and this potential is based on "Potency" in every respect i.e. eco-socio-cultural, industrial, political, S&T etc. Indirectly it is to be considered a "National Mirror" in which the statesmen can find out the capability of the country and calculate how long the country can sustain "WAR".

"Logistics" is a bridge between the aim of war and its actual conduct. And the logistic capability depends on the economic condition and industrial capacity with high-tech. "Logistic handling means handling all the means of war — Transportation-Communication Munitions Industries" [3] etc. In modern context basically war will be fought by the scientists and technocrats through their research, invention, labs. But at the same time, the 'war' would be fought by the population through their hard work in various oil deposits, industries and mines. To make one soldier capable of fighting against enemy, ten peoples have to work in various industries—like mines, fields to produce goods and commodities for conduct of war. Without active participation of the common masses war cannot be conducted successfully.[4] Therefore, it has no meaning to say easily that "war is a serious business and it should be left over to Military Generals". The nature of modern war is absolutely different, directly or indirectly every factor of a nation is involved and affected. It is apparent that without active support and participation of the population, "Logistic Management" cannot perform its expected role.

10.3 Significance and Historical Evaluation

"Logistic" is the responsibility of the war administration to procure the requirement of the combat forces with due consideration of 3R i.e. right time, right place and to the right person. And whoever had failed to follow-up strictly "3R," they were defeated by their enemy. History of warfare is a witness to it, the well-known Military Thinker Jomini explained the significance of the "Logistics-3R" in his reputed book entitled:

"Art of War" as follows:-

" For the loss of a nail a shoe was lost
For the loss of a shoe a horse was lost
For the loss of a horse a rider was lost
For the requirement of messenger a battle was lost
For the loss of battle a kingdom was lost
For the loss of "NAILS" a kingdom was lost."[5]

This example is enough to understand the significance of "3R". In a nutshell "NAIL" was a genuine reason for loosing kingdom and hence "3R" should be followed strictly by the Logistic Management.

Logistics is the lifeline for every battle, war and campaign; the history of warfare shows that whoever had casual approach or negligence towards "Logistics Management" they were the subjects of great debacle. During the third battle of Panipat—A.D.1761 Ahmed Shah Abdali strengthened his Logistics Supply and then disrupted the logistic supply line of Maratha; as a result of this successfully blockade of the Marathas, logistics by Ahmed Shah Abdali, Maratha camps were subject to severe starvation. The famine in Maratha camp was one of the genuine reasons for the defeat of Sadhashiv Rao Bhau during the third battle of Panipat[6].

During World War II, Hitler had opened the new front in North Africa against the U.K. Under the leadership of General Rommel the German Forces were landed in desert area of North Africa near Mediterranean Sea and the ultimate aim was to cut off the British "Lifeline" i.e. supply of oil, raw material from Afro-Asian colonies to Britain. [7] The ups and down or pushing back to "each other" by General Rommel and Montgomery in this desert area of North Africa were continued. The progress as well as setback was determined by "supply of fuel". Thus it is to be understood that "logistics supply" is the key element regarding successful conduct of war.

"Logistics Management" has its own significance and burden of responsibilities i.e. carry out "Movements,

Deployment and Sustained". It is to be ensured that every soldier, animal and machine must get adequate food, water, fuel, goods and commodities. Every requirement should reach at the "right" time, place and to the right person. Mobility, surprise, concentration of power, offensive action — application of these principles of war is possible only if the soldiers are properly fed. Napoleon Bonaparte said: "**An army marches on its stomach**" means unless an army is properly fed—adequately equipped to fight a war, it cannot attain the victory in war.[8]

Historical Evaluation

The "Indian Logistics" system was carried out independently. The history of Mughals shows that they had introduced independent logistics system. Mughals had their own perception that being a "Foreigner", local population will not co-operate with them, therefore, they must be self-reliant for logistics supply of the armed forces. And hence they had introduced independent logistics system. Out of fear about perfect logistics management, maximum peoples started to accompany the combat forces. In due course of time, it was found that the strength of non-combatant was more as compared to the actual combat forces. So non-combatant forces were being called "Camp Followers". This was a great cause to hamper the "mobility" of the armed forces. During third battle of Panipat, the Maratha chief of his campaign, Commander Sadhashiv Rao Bhau also had a more non-combatant (camp followers) rather than actual combat forces which was the genuine cause of great defeat of Sadhashiv Rao Bhau by Ahmed Shah Abdali: And synonymously, time to time, the defeat of the Mughals by Shivaji and the tribes/peoples of North-west frontier tract.

British also had independent arrangement for logistics supply and it was out of fear that they were foreigners. The British had visualised the practical problems and therefore introduced independent logistic management which came to be known as "Commissariat Branch". This branch was mainly responsible for procuring the requirement of the combat forces.

During World War II the Japanese had introduced a system different from that of the British to procure the requirements of the combat forces from local population. This system may cause injustice and force local residents and ultimately it may result in loosing sympathy and support from the local population. The Chinese have an independent system of logistics supply known as 'Rear Services". The rear services are entirely managed by the civilians. These services are mainly responsible to procure all the requirements of the armed forces. This Chinese logistic arrangement consisted on "Decentralisation".

India followed the independent logistics arrangement based on Decentralisation. Indian Army has various services i.e. AOC, ASC, AMC, EME. India has adopted the British system with minor rectification. The ultimate aim of this independent system of logistics is that local population should not be the subject of injustice, force, or harassment. [9]

10.4. Scope of Logistics

In "modern warfare" the scope of logistics is wider because no one can remain aloof from the actual clash. Directly or indirectly, knowingly or unknowingly every factor of a country is involved in the process of conduct of war. However, practically the scope of logistics is as follows:

1. Resources
2. Goods and commodities
3. Transportation
4. Medical

10.4.1 Resources

Basically it means Man, Means and Material. Resources do not mean allocation but "availability" of national power. Availability of military resources i.e. recruitment, training, location and mobilisation.

10.4.2 Goods and Commodities

Goods and commodities are required for the conduct of war. In military term it is war munition—Aircrafts,

Helicopters, Vehicles, Ships, Missiles; in a nutshell, the production of war material.

10.4.3 Transportation

Logistic supply means to carry out the goods and commodities from one place to another. In view of the scope of logistics transportation, the following aspects should be considered:

1. Establishment
2. Location
3. Environmental effects on transport
4. Choice of loading and unloading
5. Roads and their conditions
6. Obstacles and their nature
7. Distribution point
8. Speed and accessibility

10.4.4 Medical

As far as medical science is concerned, the study of the effects of an environment on soldiers, expected and possible diseases: Study of possible health problems of soldiers: And thorough study of hospitalisation and environmental diseases etc.[10]

10.5 Resources of Logistics

Having "resources" is a pre-requisite of logistics unless and until it is available, logistic management cannot begin their work. Basically Men, Means and Materials are being considered as the resources of logistics. The resources of logistics are as follows:

- Population
- Raw material and natural resources
- Industrial capacity
- National economy
- Agriculture development

10.5.1 Population

Population is the basic source of manpower. Population is required to conduct the war successfully with deep involvement. Population should be well disciplined with patriotic approach towards their responsibilities—whichever being assigned by the Government. It should be well trained with skill and literacy. Population is required for recruitment in the armed forces as well as employ them in various fields and sectors like munition industries for the production of war material.

10.5.2 Natural Resources and Raw Material

Natural resources is the gift given by nature and it cannot be produced by human efforts. But raw material can be produced by human efforts, and both are crucial. Only having natural resources and raw materials will not be sufficient. It has to be explored and taken out from the earth; then only it can be used for the intended purpose. If the country wishes to produce the TANKS, it must have iron deposits. Without natural resources and raw materials a country cannot produce the required war material. When it becomes a subject of economic and political control, then it becomes a notion of lifelines. e.g. the British had a lifeline, supply of oil and resources from Africa and Asia to their motherland during World War II.

10.5.3 Industrial Set-up

It would be in the interest of the country that it should have an adequate infrastructure of industrial sector. Industrial set-up of the country should be capable of producing all types of war material within the country without any foreign assistance. It is the industrial infrastructure that acts as a barometer of economic development of a nation. Industrial set-up highlights on "Production capabilities and military supply for conduct of war". Industries should be a potential contributor to the military supply i.e. arms-ammunition, aircrafts, missiles, radar, submarine, anti-aircraft guns, fire weapons, naval vessels, cargos, ships etc. [11]

10.5.4 National Economy

Logistics is the bridge between national economy and the actual conduct of war. No nation can fight the war without strong financial base. General F.C. Fuller said if you wish to conduct a war you should have: I--Money, II--Money and III--Money. First, money is required for preparation of war. For example, before launching a war, buying and dumping a fuel (oil) on a large scale is vital, without sufficient stockpile of oil, no nation can conduct a war successfully. To conduct a war heavy finance is required to maintain the continuity of "war material" production—a country has to buy strategic minerals from abroad by paying a heavy price. And third, money means even after an end of war to restore the normalcy at national level—money is essential. And as such, heavy finance is required for the reconstruction of roads, railway gauge, bridges, power stations which are normally destroyed by the enemies' bombardment during war. National economy is supposed to be strong and capable of meeting any emergency and sustain the war as long as the Government desires.

10.5.5 Agricultural Development

Agricultural development is one of the most important aspects of logistic supply. It would be always better that a country should be self-sufficient in terms of food productions. Dependency in terms of foodgrains upon other nation is considered a permanent weakness of a concerned country and subject of mercy by others. Food is highly essential for every human being. No army can sustain without food for a longer period during war. Army cannot fight the war for a longer period with empty stomach. And hence the new trend introduced in the modern war is destruction and devastation of crops in the field itself only by using chemical or biological weapons. Self sufficiency is dependent upon fertility of soil, adequate rainfall and high agro technology.[13]

10.6 Logistics Supply Chain

Logistics supply for the "Military" mainly consisted of munition industries which includes production of a variety of war materials, weapons, equipments and relevant goods and commodities i.e. conventional and non-conventional weapons like bombs, bullets missiles, shipbuilding, electronic, chemical, nuclear, automotive etc. And the production of the above war materials depends on petroleum, mining, metallurgical power and agricultural industries. This supply chain requires coordination within a national economy, labour force and national capacity.

Supply chain should be properly constituted and supposed to be easier from the mineral to goods commodities including actual user. In this supply chain re-use of waste materials, salvage, reclamation, repairing is supposed to be incorporated. It should be ensured that there should be no break-up in the constant flow of supply. The "Military Supply" is supposed to consider the following points:

Accessibility,	Schedule of distribution
Availability,	Transportation facilities
Storage points and its location,	Environmental condition
Speed and number of vehicles,	Nature of routes
Departure points,	Medical services

"Logistic supply chain" is a very crucial aspect of every combat operation. It is a lifeline for every battle which is considered as a strategic storage chain. This chain must include the maintenance and administrative aspect for man and machine i.e. soldier and his weapons and equipment while supplying the required goods-commodities, calculated tables and scales must be followed including "war wastage rate". [14] And it has to be ensured that it should reach up to FLT i.e. forward line of troops

Tentative Examples: Military Supply Chain—Indian case:

1. Army headquarter, depots and installations: Located in various parts of the country.

2. Army Maintenance Areas : Ambala Chandimandir, Jallandhar
3. Corps Maintenance Area: Pathankoat
4. Forward Maintenance Area: Jammu
5. Division Maintenance Area: Akhnoor
6. Brigade Maintenance Area: Jovina — Forward Line of troops

10.6.1 Factors of Supply chain

i) **Unity of purpose:-**All staff members and services should be treated as one — we should show that our ultimate aim is to defeat the enemy. They should have a spirit of a TEAM. Hence if the aim is similar or common, they should co-operate with everybody. Every attempt should be made to maintain cohesiveness.

ii) **Preparation:** An attempt should be made to procure the maximum requirements. Planning should be made with full preparation of resources with foresight. Preparation in every respect is supposed to be completed with presupposition and anticipation.

iii) **Economy:** Economy does not mean curtailing of resources but it's a using of resources carefully; unnecessary stocking carefully, loss and destruction or misuse of resources must be avoided.

iv) **Practicability:** Supply should be based on balance, and urgent needs. And it has to make available by groups of services. Services are supposed to be self-sufficient and sustainable to perform their responsibilities. They should not stick up with over-calculation or decided scale. In view of progress on the front, they are supposed to be flexible and the need of re-supply should not occur.

10.6.2 Functions of Logistics Supply Chain

There are four major responsibilities as far as guidelines for supply chain is concerned:

1. Planning and its execution
2. Deal with vigilance from base to forward post
3. Appropriate treatment to all
4. Maintenance

Four-fold functions of logistic supply chain

1) **Design and development:** Evacuation and disposition of material.
2) **Personal Care:** Attention at personal level should be paid which will be helpful to maintain the relationship and emotional attachment.
3) **Facilities:** Maximum facilities to be provided i.e. transport, accommodation construction and repairing.
4) **Services:** As a part of legal and moral duty, services to the combat branches should be made available. Medical, catering, supply of ammunition to the right person at the right time and at the right place.[15]

10.7 Principles of Logistics Management

To procure the requirement of the combat forces at the "Right time, right place and to the right person" is the primary responsibility of the logistic management. In this modern warfare logistic management has to play a very crucial role with wider perspective. Without "unity of efforts" by the various branches of logistics and combat forces, war cannot be conducted and won successfully. Within the variety of services this Organisation has to work smoothly; therefore, certain principles have to be followed strictly by the logistics management. The principles of logistics management are as follows:

- Co-operation
- Simplicity
- Flexibility
- Economy
- Foresight

10.7.1 Co-operation

Co-operation is one of the principles of war, it has been said that without co-operation no operation is possible. It means that co-operation is required within the various services of logistics and combat branches. Everybody should understand the limitations and problems of each others. The combat forces authorities should intimate about their expected requirements well in advance. Authorities of logistic management should also understand the significance of time. Once the sense of unity and integrity to defeat the enemy is developed, feelings of vigorous co-operation will be automatically generated.

10.7.2 Simplicity

Inequalities is a natural phenomenon; even five fingers of our palm are not similar. Synonymously all soldiers, officers working in the combat and non-combat branches of the armed forces are not of the same nature. This logistics channel-structure should be easier and simple to understand. There should be no complicated procedure or pattern to work in the logistics supply channel.[16] It is to be ensured that anyone can work smoothly without any ambiguity or confusion.

10.7.3 Flexibility

It means potency to copeup with variable circumstances. During armed confrontation things will not occur according to our expectation. Everybody should be mentally and physically prepared to adjust with the new situation during war. Logistics authorities are supposed to be flexible regarding distribution of resources i.e. supply. Every time they are not expected to follow the "ratio of supply". According to progress on the front the demand may be increased and hence the logistics authorities have to consider and prepare themselves to be "flexible".[17]

10.7.4 Economy

Economy of the efforts, is one of the "principles of war". Whatever national resources are available for the conduct of war it should be used with an economy point of view. Everybody should keep in mind that every bullet, vehicle, weapon, goods, commodities are precious assets of the country and it should not be misused. Unnecessary use or wastage must be prevented carefully. Economy does not mean unnecessary crunch or curtailing of resources but to ensure that resources should be economically used. For example, if the vehicle is not working it should be repaired at the earliest so that it can resume the previous services.

10.7.5 Foresight

It means preparing the plan in order to cope up with unpredicted situation. During war many things will be against our plan or expectation. Logistics management has to anticipate negative development and be prepared to substitute arrangements well in advance.

For example, if the water storage is being destroyed by enemy's air attack, then what are the options? On the basis of presupposition of such unexpected incident, alternative arrangement has to be made. Non-availability of water, fuel, food, ammunition may affect negatively on the process of conduct of war. And, therefore, planners of logistic supply should have a foresight. [18]

10.8 Factors Affecting on Logistics During War

a) **Operational Plan:** To conduct the operation it is highly essential to decide the objective. Once the objective is determined, then only composition of troops could be finalised. The composition of troops should have relevance to the "objective". While planning for combat operation wastage rate should be considered and order of battle has to be analysed and understood properly.

b) **Enemy's Threat:** Threats and types of threat will decide the location. And then accordingly nature of dumping of goods and commodities will be finalised. Threat perception is most important; once the threat perception is cleared then location of stockpiling will be finalised.

c) **Maintenance of Communication:** From rear zone to combat sector, assignments to the combat units should be finalised. The requirements of communication are to be identified and at the same time the nature of transportation to be finalised. The transportation and communication should be maintained up to FLT i.e. forward line of troops.

d) **Terrain:** Nature of terrain will decide the course of logistic management action. It will depend on nature whether it is a jungle, plain, desert or a place at high altitude and if it is a high altitude, then dropping zone will have to be prepared. So it is terrain which will decide the course of action for logistics management.

e) **Climate**: Local climate will affect the consumption, number of casualties and load carrying capacity by 20%. And oxygen to the bodies will be required.

f) **Local Resources:** Logistics management can minimise its burden by availing of maximum resources from local place i.e. fresh ration, water, timber construction material, labour force, hospital and workshop facilities etc. can be managed at local level.

g) **Local Populations:** In the modern war local population of the border area particularly can play a supporting role for logistics supply. Local population can provide accommodation facilities, assist for transportation, and even local population can be employed for labour work and sabotage activities against enemy.[19]

10.9 Logistics Planning

Logistics planning raises the number of questions and queries i.e. where-when-what and how? It is to be remembered that the logistic planning factors are numerical values which represent the quantitative relationship that exist between the composition and the deployment of military forces and available material facilities.

General factors for logistics planning are as follows:

- Availability of required resources
- Utilisation of materials
- Planning of supply at various levels

- Distance
- Number of units
- Transportation
- Repairing (workshop)
- Salvage and hospitalisation
- Weapons and equipments
- Communication
- Construction
- Raw material and natural resources
- Time

Mobilisation: Military logistics is the supply of means and materials and rendering of services to the operating military forces. Whereas the civil logistics means the mobilisation of industries and economic resources in order to support the armed forces. War mobilisation is vital for "logistic planning"; without mobilisation process resources in maximum numbers cannot be made available. Mobilisation means gearing up the resources by preventing misuse of economy.

As far as "war mobilisation process" is concerned, only control over wastage and misuse of resources will not produce the expected result. In addition to economic and industrial resources there are numbers of measures to be adopted to mobilise the resources; for example, controlling the resources by rationing. There are many intangible aspects such as leadership, administration, strategic foresight etc. which can be the supporting factors for mobilisation of resources.

Once the process of mobilisation is started at the domestic front and maximum resources are made available, then planning at various levels can be made. For example, planning at industrial transportation and medical level may be chalked out tentatively.

Logistics Planning — Factors to be considered

Industrial	Transportation	Medical
1) Requirements by Combat forces	1) Location of delivery points	1) Study of nature of terrain
2) Available raw material & Strategic Minerals	2) Available routes & substitute routes in case of emergency	2) Expected health problem & diseases
3) Available manpower & required extra manpower	3) Numbers of vehicles available	3) Available medicines, doctors nurses & beds
4) Power Supply	4) Workshop arrangements for repairing & maintenance	4) Transportation means
5) Schedule of production	5) Time— from Departure point to delivery point	
6) Given time limit	6) Possibly required vehicles in addition to available vehicles etc	
7) Transportation for delivery		

Expected Problems: During conduct of war "Transportation" for "Logistics" has to be kept in a perfect manner. Taking into consideration variable geographical condition area wise jungle, desert, high altitude and plain — logistics management has to work accordingly. Apart from the logistic problems in various terrains, the logistics management has to cope with the situation by facing the following problems:

1. During the process of transportation i.e. on road, if suddenly a concerned vehicle meets with an accident, then "time" factor affects.

2. Logistic vehicles have always been the subject of destruction by enemy's attack.
3. Technician-Engineers-workers are supposed to work with risk during war.
4. During skirmishes even the medical services i.e. doctors, nurses are supposed to provide treatment to the wounded soldiers. And some time even Medical Camp/ Hospital also becomes a subject of bombing during war. So during logistic planning process the above unexpected—problems are to be considered well in advance.

Footnotes

1. Louis C. Peltier and G. Etzel Pearcy, *Military Geography,* East West Press, Madras, 1981, p.72.
2. Precis on *Logistics Management,* Department of Defence and Strategic Studies, University of Pune, Pune 7, 1982.
3. Brig. Pramodh Sarin, Retd., *Military Logistics: The Third Dimension,* Manas Publications, New Delhi, 2000, pp. 14-15.
4. Edward Mead Earle, *Makers of Modern Strategy,* Natraj Publishers, Dehradun, 2003, pp. 280-90.
5. Major Jodh Singh, Retd., *War Its Principles, Tactics and Strategies,* Surjeet Publication, 7K, Kolhapur Road, Kamla Nagar, Delhi, 1980, p. 95.
6. GP.Capt, Retd., S.G. Chitnis and Lt. Retd., A.P. Choudhary, *Indian Military History,* Archana Publication, Jalgaon, 1985, pp. 67-69.
7. Louis C. Peltier and G. Etzel Pearcy, *op. cit.,* p.75.
8. Major Jodh Singh, Retd, *op. cit.,* p. 95.
9. Lt.Col.M.G.Abhyankar, Retd., *Defence Principles and Organisation,* Usha Prakashan, Ganeshkhind, Pune 7, 1974, pp. 159-60.
10. Precis on *Logistics Management,* D.D.S.S, 1982, University of Pune, *op. cit.,* 1982.

11. Louis C. Peltier and G. Etzel Pearcy, *op. cit.*, pp. 73-75.
12. Brig. Parmodh Sarin, Retd, *op. cit.*, pp.188-90.
13. R.L. Dwivedi, *Fundamentals of Political Geography*, Chaitanya Publishing House, University Road, Allahabad, 1990, pp. 88-89.
14. Louis C. Peltier and G. Etzel Pearcy, *op. cit.*, pp. 78-81.
15. Precis on *Logistics Management*, D.D.S.S., Pune, *op.cit.*
16. Lt. Col. M. G. Abhyankar, Retd., *op. cit.*, pp. 161-62.
17. Brig. Parmodh Sarin, Retd., *op. cit.*, pp. 77-79.
18. Lt.Col.M.G. Abhyankar, Retd., *op. cit.*, pp.161-62.
19. Precis on *Logistics, op. cit.*, Pune.
20. Brig. Parmodh Sarin, Retd., *op. cit.*, pp.169-72. *See also* Louis C. Peltier and G. Etzel Pearcy, *op. cit.*, pp. 81-85.

✣ ✣ ✣

11

STRATEGIC IMPORTANCE OF INDIA'S LAND AND MARITIME BOUNDARIES

11. INTRODUCTION

India occupies a significant position in Asia and world politics. Air routes of world's air traffic passes through Indian air space. And important maritime trade traffic passing via Arabian Sea and Bay of Bengal is the subject of India's maritime boundaries. [1] Since ancient period India has well reputation as a "land of resources". In the past aggressors and invaders were attracted by the fabulous wealth of India. The invaders had a "strong determination" and hence neither the plains of Punjab, desert of Rajasthan and nor a difficult terrain of Northwest frontier tract forbade them to enter and plunder India. The Dutch, the British and the French had arrived at the Western Sea Coast of India and took due advantages and finally India became part of "British Empire". India's "land boundaries" and its safety, security and territorial integrity were challenged by the enemy from time to time. The great Himalayas also failed to act as a "Natural Barrier" against China.[2] Despite having contradiction in geographical setting of borders, Pakistan attacked India four times. Skirmishes between security forces of India and Bangladesh are a common phenomenon. It can be concluded on the basis of above facts that India's land boundaries had never been unchallenged.

11.1.2 Historical Evaluation

India's northern boundary had never been demarcated on the actual ground due to its difficult nature of terrain; Indo-Myanmar boundary was determined on the basis of Patkoi ranges and poses no political stress. It is the Peoples Republic of China who has rejected to consider the Himalayan ranges as a natural boundary. As far as Indo-Bangladesh land boundary is concerned, it poses certain problems and in due course of time would be sorted out. Regarding India's western land boundary it has contiguity with Pakistan by having contradicting geographical setting. The Indo-Pak boundary was determined by Radcliff award with certain 'discrepancies' and ambiguities which culminated in boundary and territorial disputes. Radcliff Commission and especially Sir Cyril Radcliff failed to draw the geopolitically accurate boundary. Even Sir Henry McMahon determined the boundary between Tibet and Assam (Arunachal Pradesh) on paper in 1914 which also has discrepancies and ambiguity. It is apparent that the British had sown the seeds of long term border tension, boundary and territorial disputes over Aksai-chin and Kashmir for India and her neighbours. Sir Cyril Radcliff was assisted by two boundary commissions i.e. India-Pakistan including east and west Pakistan. It is to be noted that Sir Radcliff did not deal with the boundary of Jammu and Kashmir as it was a princely state by that time. But whatever delimitation and demarcation was done under his leadership till today, it has remained a constant irritant and hurdle and source of conflict between India, Pakistan and now Bangladesh.[3]

While carrying out an evaluation of India's land boundaries, we should consider the border area, nature of terrain, population, means of communication, status of development, geostrategic importance and defence problems. For evaluation purpose India's land border can be categoriesed into three major parts:

1) Western land boundary
2) Northern land boundary
3) North-eastern land boundary

11.1.3 India's Western Land Boundary

India's western land boundary was demarcated on actual ground under the leadership of Sir Cyril Radcliff which poses numbers of critical problems. The study of this India's western land boundary has to be carried out into two parts:

A) International Boundary

B) Line of Actual Control

A) International Boundary: This boundary has physical contiguity with Pakistan: Starting from the extreme west, there were four Indian states having physical contiguity with Indo-Pak boundary i.e. Gujarat, Rajasthan, Punjab and Jammu and Kashmir. The total length of this I.B. is 3127 (approx) kms.

i) Gujarat Sector : This boundary begins from Rann of Kutch (near Sir Creek) and goes towards the Punjab, near Rani Ka Bera village. The total length of this Gujarat sector is 508 kms. The peoples of this territory are peace-loving by nature and business oriented.[4] Maximum population belongs to Hindu-Gujrati, Muslims. But in border area most of them are Muslims and have contact with the other side. The area is flat and smooth like a table top; for near about eight months, the ground is firm and accessible by tanks and armoured personal vehicles but as soon as monsoon starts, the entire area gets flooded by sea and rain water. The well-known Rann of Kutch area has a quicksand and it's of a different kind than that of Rajasthan. In this sector Pakistan has advantages, from operational point of view, because on their side the area is situated on higher elevation and is not subject to flooding except in monsoon. This land is an open invitation for tank warfare. From cultivation point of view, this land is not so feasible but by virtue of high agro-technology, some of the area is being developed as a "Green Belt" by border security force.[5] We can realise the contrast in temperature —during day it is extreme hot and at night it is severe cold. It is difficult to get drinking water in this border area. In ancient period this land had been very rich, Mohammed Gazni had invaded Somnath temple of Gujarat and collected huge wealth from it. During 1965 war of India and Pakistan, "Rann of Kutch" was an area of conflict. Some of the portions of this area were given by India to Pakistan as a part of respect to International Tribunal. [6] From strategic point of view Gujarat State is an important one, which is linked with the Arabian Sea. It is a prosperous state, by having good rainfall, fertility of soil, and contribution towards national economy. Pakistani I.S.I agents are trying to mount up the communal tension between the Hindu and the Muslim community in this area.

Pakistan has already claimed over Sir Creek area of the Arabian Sea. The well-known Bombay High now Mumbai High also situated in the Arabian Sea, is the source of oil and natural gas for India. This territory can be the gateway to have an accession with Indian Ocean. The territory is rich in terms of "Resources".

ii) **Rajasthan Sector:** Proceeding from "Rani Ka Bera" village, this boundary passes through the historical state i.e. Rajasthan, having the length of 1037 kms. The four districts Ganganagar, Bikaner, Jaisalmer and Barmer lie along this Indo-Pak boundary. As per geographical description, the Rajasthan sector is a "Great Indian Desert" like Gujarat sector and the temperature is critical during night being extreme cold and during day it is unbearably hot.

Adequate water is not available, so scarcity of water is a peculiar problem for human being in the

Rajasthan sector. The whole area is a vast sandy one alongwith high sand dunes. When Mohammed Gazni had sacked on sorti Somnath temple of Gujarat, he had access through Rajasthan to maintain the secrecy of this sack.[7]

The density of population is low and scattered in numbers of group. Famine exists for years together and the population migrates to other states with their cattle during summer. There is a large percentage of Muslims in this border area. Amongst the Rajputs one can find sodha Rajputs who are living in Pakistan as well. This is a land of gallant warriors who had done heroic deeds in the past. It should be acknowledged that it was the Rajputs from this soil who had checked the Islamic invasion time to time in the past.[8] During 1971 Indo-Pak War, the well-known battle of Longanwala was fought in the sand hills of the western part of Jaisalmer. The popular movie "Border" by director J.P. Datta was centric to this "Battle of Longawala".

By virtue of science and technology the face of this state is changed after 1971 war, but the tactical problems remain as they are. Dispersed operations are an ideal for this desert belt. The deployment of large bodies of troops becomes a difficult task due to shortage of water. The road systems are primitive except the strategic roads constructed by joint venture of Border Road Organisation and General Reserve Engineering Force. Army manoeuvre is feasible during winter and summer whereas scarcity of water is a hazard. Water well, storage, holds a strategic importance during war in the desert. It has been said that "blood is cheap but water is costly". This area is well connected by railway lines, roads and air transportation. The deposits of oil and natural gas are also found in this state which is one of the cheap source of energy production and holds strategic importance.

iii) **Punjab Sector:** This western land boundary of India passes through the Punjab State with a length of 533 kms. This area of border is a plain and flat area which offers an extreme mobility for the combat forces. The territory is served by rivers, canals and has good road and railway network on both sides. It is well reputed for fertile soil, good rainfall and its resourcefulness. It is one of the developed states of India and has a great contribution for national economy. Except monsoon this territory is suitable for combat operation. It has a great tradition of gallant warriors. In the past numbers of decisive battles had been fought on this soil like Mahabharata, battle of Sobraon, battle of Terrain etc. The population comprises Sikhs, Jats, Rajputs, Hindus and Muslims. The Sikhs are in majority and on the other side, Sikhs and Punjabi Musalmans. The people of this soil have a great contribution towards services in the Indian armed forces and various sectors of the country.

The wars of 1965 and 1971 had fought very grimly as the land is extremely accessible and offers "mobility". Opposite to this sector is the triangular heartland of Pakistan i.e. trijunction of three districts, Multan, Sargodha and Lahore. During 1965 conflict, Indian forces advanced and reached very close to Lahore. It is said that Pakistan has constructed Ichogil canal to be a hazard for enemy and this purpose was fulfilled during 1965 war when the Indian forces halted near Ichogil canal and could not proceed for Lahore. From Amritsar the location of International Boundary is only 34 kms away and from this I.B. is eleven kilometers across the Pakistani city where "Lahore" is situated.[9] In view of the strategic significance of her triangular heartland in the eighties, Pakistan tried to create independent buffer state between India and

Pakistan i.e. "Khalistan" by misguiding the peoples and cultivating terrorism in Punjab. But owing to due attention and appropriate measures by the Government of India, the dream of Pakistan was brushed off. In view of the significance of this sector and previous experience Pakistani forces are concentrated in the area opposite to Punjab sector. Taking into consideration of changing political climate and positive developments in Indo-Pak relations, very soon historical rail-road link would be re-established. The well-known "model"of smooth functioning i.e. 'Wagha Check Post" also is located in this sector.

iv) **Jammu and Kashmir Sector:** The IB after leaving Punjab passes through 'J & K' state having a length of 199 kms. This IB starts from village of Burejal—where the line of actual control ends—and runs upto the Madavpur bridge on the Ravi River near Pathankoat. Jammu is 11 kms away from this IB and Pakistani city Sialkot is only 8 kms away. The entire area of this sector receives adequate rainfall. In terms of cultivation this soil is very fertile and rich for fruits and dry fruits production. Actually this territory of Kashmir is heaven on this earth by having tremendous natural beauty and potential of income-oriented foodgrains and resources. This territory has been a subject of attraction, invasion and domination by rulers since ancient period and one of the points of escalation between India and Pakistan.[10] The population of the entire Kashmir and Gilgit valley is dominated by Muslims and Pundits, Jammu by Hindus and Ladakh by Buddhists. This area is covered by mountains and forests with narrow and deep valleys. From tactical point of view the terrain is very difficult for security forces but very ideal and suitable for the enemy to carry out terrorist, insurgent and guerrilla activities.

> During heavy monsoon, landslide poses transportation problems. In this difficult terrain transportation, communication and logistic supply is a great headache for the security forces. Due to heavy snowfall the passes get blocked during winter. From the strategic point of view, this sector has a great significance. It is located in the north of India and is bound by Tibet in the east and Sinkiang province of China in the north. To its west is Afghanistan and to the South-west is Pakistan. According to the hidden agenda of America they are interested to create another Israel in South-Asian region. The three different civilisations has physical contiguity with this sector i.e. Hindu, Muslim, Buddhist, and Sikh with three different ideology i.e. theocratic-military dictatorship in Pakistan, communism in China and democracy in India.

From economic point of view this state is very rich. We can see the major rivers, vegetation, crops, fruits, dry fruits, tourism—the best sources of economic prosperity.[11] But since 1947-48 it has been the source of conflict and battlefield for "Proxy war" due to consecutive defeat of Pakistan. From 27th of July 1949, the day of ceasefire, Pakistan is continuing to illegally occupying Kashmir and lays its claim over the whole state of Jammu and Kashmir and hence does not recognise even the well-determined international boundary line in this sector.

B) Line of Actual Control: (sketch no.6)

The term "Line of Actual Control" clears that the "Kashmir Issue" is yet to be settled between India and Pakistan. The total length of the line of actual control including Siachen Glacier area is 850 kms, approximately. It starts from a point little north of Kargil and goes west till Tithwal from where it turns south. It continues southward and halts near the village of Burejal where it meets the Indo-Pak I.B.

It was October 1947 that Raja Hari Singh was deeply involved in celebrating Dasshera function. Pakistan had sent the infiltrators and soldiers in civilian dress and tried to grab Kashmir. But, once it was merged with India on 27th October 1947, immediately the Indian armed forces came into action. So this conflict was brought to an end by the effort of UN observer and the ceasefire line between India and Pakistan troops came into existence with effect from 27th July 1949. After Indo-Pak war of 1971, this line instead of ceasefire line came to be recognised as a Line of Actual Control with minor changes. The UN passed the resolution to be implemented by both India and Pakistan but it is apparent that practically both the countries are reluctant to execute the UN resolution.

Pakistan has occupied illegally 78,114 kms territory of Kashmir comprising Gilgit, Muzaffarabad, Rawalkot, Mirpur Koti and Bhimber. The occupied area is known as "Pakistan occupied Kashmir" (POK). Kashmir under the control of India is known as Azad Kashmir. Some of the military bases situated to the east of this line are occupied by India—Poonch Mendhar, Naoshahra etc. (**sketch no.6**)

This line of Actual Control passes through the most difficult mountainous terrain and dense forest which creates a number of defence-oriented problems.[12] We can see the conflict between determinism and possibilism, how nature is cruel and human being trying to have an "upperhand" over nature. Crores of rupees have been spent in this territory by both the countries by neglecting other developmental activities within their respective countries. Despite passing a span of 60 years, this problem of Kashmir is yet to be settled and remained an escalation point in their bilateral relations. At present political climate has changed and both the countries seems to be kind enough to think and act in a co-operative manner for the welfare of the peoples of both the side of the Line of Actual Control. Like re-establishing the transportation services which they had before 1947—introducing relief points for the victims of earthquake, declaring ceasefire-peace in this area of the Line of Actual Control etc.

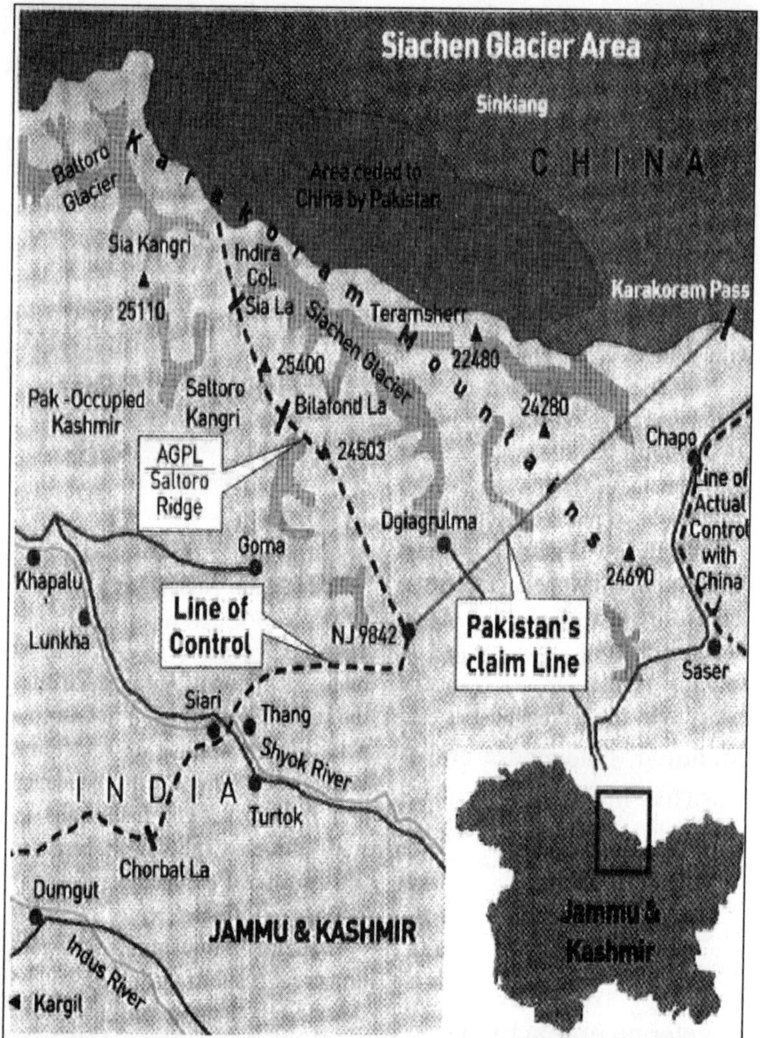

Indian troops are deployed on the Actual Ground Position Line from the end of NJ 9842 to Indira Col. Pakistan claims the area from NJ 9842 to the Karakoram Pass. A line running straight from NJ 9842 to the northern border with China would be a fair compromise.

Sketch No. 6: **Line of Actual Control, Pak Occupied Kashmir and Siachen Glacier**

Source : "Frontline", 22-04-06

MAP NOT TO SCALE

11.1.4 Northern Land Boundary

Preamble: India's northern land boundary passes through the Himalayas. This mighty Himalayas is spread over a number of sovereign states i.e. Afghanistan, Pakistan, India, Nepal, Bhutan (Tibet), China, Myanmar etc. India shares the maximum long boundary with China and then Nepal, Bhutan. India's boundary with China begins from Kashmir in the north-west along the Himalayan ranges upto the Tri-Junctions of Myanmar, China and India near the Talu pass in Arunachal Pradesh.[13] This "Northern Boundary" of India is the second longest land boundary in the world having a total length of 6506 kms including Nepal and Bhutan. Being the oldest boundary it also poses socio-cultural, historical problems in addition to "defence problems". This northern boundary had never been demarcated on the actual ground due to critical geographical circumstances. The area is exceedingly rugged with inaccessible mountains and deep gorges. There are 128 minor and major passes in the Himalayas and it is very difficult even to reach at some places. Poor visibility, inaccessibility, complex nature had added the misconception and perception which culminated in military confrontation in 1962.[14] While studying the geographical circumstances, population, resources, strategic importance, defence problems, it is vital to be aware about the facts relevant to Geostrategic perspective.

11.1.5 Geostrategic Perspectives

1. China has already illegally occupied 38,000 sq.kms of Indian territory in Aksai-Chin besides about 5,180 sq.kms of Indian territory ceded by Pakistan to China. China already constructed KaraKoram Highway to have an access with Pakistan via Kashmir.[15]

2. China has not only objected about the validity of McMahon line but also claims 94,700 sq.kms of territory in Arunachal Pradesh owing only to its "Resource Potential".[16] According to Geological survey of India coal, oil, dolomite, phosphite is found in Arunachal

Pradesh. At present five oil wells have been successfully sunk by oil India Ltd in the Kharsang area of Tirap district of Arunachal Pradesh. In view of these resources and two international tri-junction points, China claims over Arunachal Pradesh.[17] **(sketch no.7)**

3. China adopted "Strategic encirclement" policy against India, which begins from KaraKoram highway, Aksai Chin, the Sino-Indian border, Myanmar and down to the Bangladesh, Bay of Bengal.[18]
4. From Indian side, roads and communication and required infrastructure are inadequate to meet the Chinese threat in future. But China has already undertaken the nuclearisation, modernisation and militarisation programme in Tibet.[19] In the near future strong China would be more rough and tough negotiator. India's boundary dispute with China is yet to be settled and hence it should be taken seriously.
5. India's northern border area is very rich in terms of natural resources and raw material. In addition to Arunachal Pradesh, the rest of the area also have a lot of natural resources, raw material and strategic minerals which are highly essential for industrial and economic development as well as defence preparedness of the country.
6. China has already constructed a road from Sinkiang to western Tibet through AksaiChin (Indian territory). This road is most important for the Chinese from the strategic point of view. [20]

The study of India's northern boundary is a crucial task and this study can be carried out into three parts:

a) Western Sector: Ladakh and Himachal Pradesh

b) Central Sector: Uttarakhand and Nepal

c) Eastern Sector: Sikkim, Bhutan and Arunachal Pradesh

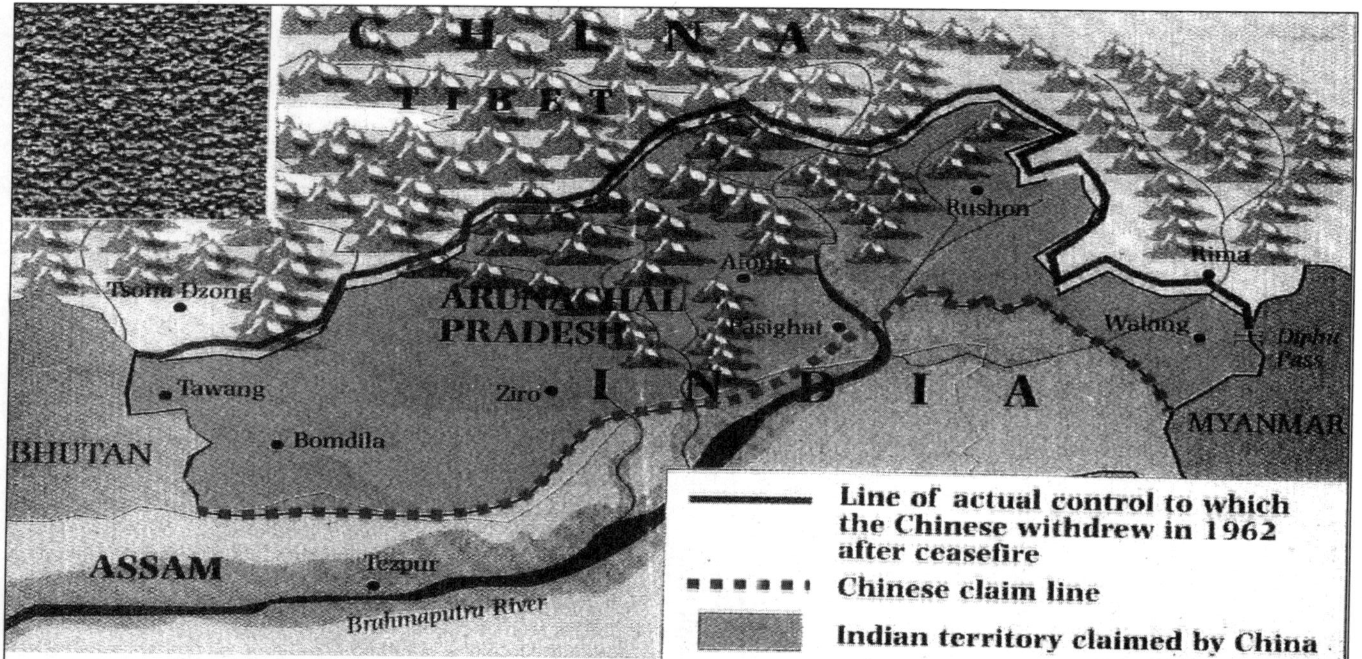

Sketch No. 7: **Chinese Claim Over Arunachal Pradesh**

Source : Dr. M. L. Sali "India China Border Dispute", Ashish Publishing Corporation New Delhi, 1998

MAP NOT TO SCALE

a) Western Sector: (sketch no. 8)

Ladakh—The Ladakh region of Jammu and Kashmir has contiguity with Sinkiang and Tibet. This boundary has a length of 560 kms alongwith the mighty Himalayan ranges on its north and east Ladakh being guarded by the Hindukush and KaraKoram mountains on the west and north. The well-known Aksai Chin and Pakistan-occupied Kashmir is also a part of this western sector. Aksai-Chin declared as a "disputed territory" by China and it grabbed maximum portion during 1954-62. The terrain is very difficult for accessibility and for even developmental activities. Transportation is very difficult—the maximum portion of the terrain is occupied by barren land, chains of the mountains and deep and narrow valleys.[21] The population basically belongs to Buddhist religion in majority. The people of this region have mixed ethnic stock; they belong to "Tibetan, and Indo-Mongoloid" strain. From strategic point of view, this Ladakh sector is most important. The presence of Pakistan and China in POK and Aksai Chin and their strategic cooperation i.e. KaraKoram Highway via Khunjerao pass is a great challenge for India's security management. According to Geological Survey of India gold, uranium, and salt can be found in this area. Both the adversaries, Pakistan and China grabbed the Indian Territory which is declared as a disputed territory. From defence point of view the important passes located here, are Karakoram, Qisil, Jilga and Lanak La etc.[22] In view of defence preparedness, India has to be more vigilant while emphasis should be on "Mountaineering warfare". This boundary constitutes the watershed between the Indus system in India and the Khotan system in China. But China has already rejected to accept "watershed principle" for the settlement of boundary dispute. China has constructed highway through Indian territory with a view to establish link between Sinkiang and western Tibet. This is one of the strategic roads for the Chinese, through which they can control the restlessness of Tibet and employ the forces whenever they required.

Sketch No. 8: **Aksai Chin** *Source* : "Frontline", 20th Oct. 2006

MAP NOT TO SCALE

Himachal Pradesh: After leaving Ladakh this boundary passes through Himachal Pradesh. The total length is 300kms with two major passes i.e. Kaurik and Shipki. This area is inhabited by Lahulies who are Buddhist having religious ties with Ladakhis. They treat "Lhasa" as a religious Headquarter. In addition to the Buddhists, Hindu population also are existing and they have their own "Village God".[23] The two districts of this state are Kinnaur and Lahul and Spiti. This border region is occupied by forest and high altitudes of 16000 ft to 21000 ft. The well-known Tibetan leader Dalai Lama took asylum at Dharamshala and operates an exile Government from this soil of Himachal Pradesh (India). In this area passes are most difficult with forest and altitudes and communications are being improved with great difficulty. This border area has a lot of natural resources, raw material and minerals. Natural gas is already found and this land is fit for horticulture.[24] The overall terrain is difficult to establish smoothly transportation and communication—it is a great challenge. This area is very critical and poses a number of problems for logistics. To defend this territory only jungle and high altitude warfare can be worked out.

b) Central Sector

Uttarakhand: This territory was a part of a Uttar Pradesh and now has separate identity as Uttarakhand, one of the states of Indian Union. This boundary lies on the water parting between the Sutlej and Kali, Alaknanda and the Bhagirathi. This watershed boundary passes through a number of passes and districts—Mana, Niti, Kungri Bingri, Tunjuna La and Lipulekh, Uttarkashi, Chamoli, Pithorgarh, Garhwal, Almora districts while sharing the border with Tibet and Nepal. In this area Hindu, Muslim and Buddhist population co-exist but particularly in mountain regions like Pahari, Rajput, Gurkha dominates the area. The Pahari-speaking Hindus of this state share the culture as north India and basically they are Indo-Aryans and emigrated from Central Asia.[25]

This area offers a number of challenges to security management. Accessibility and tactical manoeuvre is difficult. This border area is covered by dense forest, rock, and snow-covered mountains.

Nepal: After leaving Uttarakhand this Himalayan boundary runs along the sovereign and independent state of Nepal. Indo-Nepal boundary was drawn up on the basis of Sanganli treaty in A.D. 1815 and Anglo-Nepalese treaty of A.D. 1921 and successfully demarcated on the ground. The plains of Uttarakhand and Bihar run into the plains of Nepal. The total length of Indo-Nepal boundary is 1751kms (approx).

Nepal has buffer location between two powerful belligerent with different ideology i.e. India and China. The people of Nepal are of mixed ethnic stock-Tibetan, Indo-Mongoloid, Tibeto-Mongoloid etc. The population is divided into various groups like Bhotias, Tamangs Limbus, Rais, Sherpas, Hindus, Muslims and Buddhists.[27] India has special rights as a part of treaty of friendship but this treaty has been a subject of rift in Indo-Nepal relation. It is apparent that Nepalies have been attracted towards China as compared to India as China has given more assistance to Nepal. In near future Nepal may act as a puppet of the Chinese. Nepal is now being intensively used by the ISI of Pakistan to carry out anti-Indian activities while on account of open Indo-Nepal border there were no effective barrier for infiltration, terrorist and saboteurs to India.

According to survey carried out along the Indo-Nepal border area it has come out that Islamic movement is well proliferated. There are 343 mosques, 330 madrasas and 17 mosque-cum-madrasas within 10 kms of border on the Indian site. And on the Nepal side there are 282 mosques, 181 madrasas and 8 mosques cum madrasas. [28] It is not an allegation but a bitter truth that behind the shield of Islamic movement the ISI of Pakistan is working for anti-Indian activities.

c) Eastern Sector

Sikkim:- After passing Nepal this boundary runs along Sikkim by 225 kms. It follows the watershed, the crest of the mountain ranges separating the water and flowing into the Sikkim Teesta and it's affluence from the water flowing into the Tibetan Machu and Northwards into other rivers in Tibet. Nearly two-third of Sikkim consists of very high mountains, perpetually covered with snow from glacier and villages are situated generally, between the altitude of 1000 to 2000 meters on river terraces and gradual slopes. Sikkim is inhabited by Bhotias and Tibetans. They have very high respect about Dalai Lama and consider Lhasa as a piligrim centre.This population belongs to Buddhist religion and are followers of Lamaist Buddhist.[29]

Before 1974 Sikkim was an independent State but now Sikkim is an Indian State. The Sikkim boundary is the only boundary which was demarcated on actual ground successfully as a part of Anglo-Chinese convention of 1890. Some of the important passes being situated on this border area i.e. Gora La, Nathu La and Julep La. Maximum portion of lower Sikkim is mainly occupied by forest. This area has adequate natural wealth which is a source of raw material. In addition to this, some minerals can be found in this area. Between the western border of Sikkim and the western border of Bhutan, there is a strip of land Chumbi Valley [31] shaped like a dagger with its point towards India. Nathu La Pass is one of the points for border trade between India and China.

Mao Tse Tung once upon a time said that "Arunachal Pradesh, Sikkim, Bhutan, Nepal and Ladakh are the five fingers of the Chinese Palm". [32] This may be the reason why Chinese were interested to introduce the Nathu La Pass as one of the points for border trade. We are well prepared to defend our border. In 1967 Nathu La Pass was the subject of Chinese attack but it was defended gallantly by Indian forces. Governments of India and China introduced a border trade point in this sector. Government of India introduced a "special Mountaineering Division" to deal with northern border. Strategically this area is most important.

Bhutan: Northern boundary of India runs through Bhutan—an independent and sovereign state—with whom India has a special treaty relations. The Indo-Bhutanese boundary was developed as a result of the Sincha La pass treaty which was concluded in 1865. [33] The boundary alignment has been demarcated by stone pillars and poses no political stress with India.

The people of this area are Bhotias and they are from Tibetan stock and look towards Lhasa as a religious Head-quarter and Dalai Lama as spiritual leader. Like Sikkimese they are Lamaist Bhuddists.[34] The location of Bhutan between the Tibetan plateau and Assam-Bengal plains of India made it strategically important. Assam and Sikkim have a common border with Bhutan. The traditional Sino-Bhutan boundary extends to 500 kilometers and follows the crest of the Himalayas.[35] The Bhutanis feel insecure and finds themselves in an embarrassing position between the two belligerents countries of India and China.

Arunachal Pradesh: This northern boundary of India runs from the 24th state of India, Arunachal Pradesh. It is surrounded by Bhutan in the west and Tibet and China in the southeast. This boundary has been established along the Himalayan crest of the northern watershed of Brahmaputra, except where the Lohit, Dihang, Subansiri and Nyamijang rivers break through that watershed. This boundary runs from the eastern limit of Bhutan to a point near the Talu pass at the trijunction of India, Tibet and Myanmar, with a length of 1140 Kms.[36]

The population of this border area is basically tribal and scattered into numbers of tribes and sub-tribes. They belong to Mongoloid race and distinctly from four main groups of Nagas, Abors, Daflas and Bhotias. Some of the tribes emigrated from Tibet and settled in this area. Therefore, we can find some of the similarities between Arunachalis and Tibetans due to similar religion and ethnic stocks.[37]

After 1962 India had concentrated to improve the transportation and communication network in this area. The Border Road Organisation and General Reserve Engineering Force — BRO and GREF — put every possible effort to meet the requirements of the security forces for transportation and communication as compared to China. Our network of transportation and communication is satisfactory but some of the networks are yet to develop. [38]

This boundary between Tibet (China) and Arunachal Pradesh was delimited on the paper at tri-Party conference held in 1914 at Shimla. The British officer, Secretary to the political department, Sir Henry McMahon, took the initiative to determine this boundary. From strategic point of view, this territory is one of the most important. This territory has the two tri-junction points which also have international importance, i.e. Bhutan, China and India to the west and Myanmar, China (Tibet) and India to the east. This territory has vast deposits of natural resources, minerals and raw materials. Oil deposits have been found and a number of minerals have been the subject of exploitation. This region receives good rainfall and the soil is very fertile.[39] In view of the resourceful features of this territory and strategic location China has claimed possession of Arunachal Pradesh and declared it as a disputed territory. The high altitudes and jungle have forced our armed forces to be prepared for jungle and high altitude warfare.

11.1.5 North-East Land Boundary (sketch no.9)

1. **Preamble:** The North-East region of India is most important for a number of reasons. This region has been divided into seven states by having multi-language culture, ethnic stock and religion. Geostrategically this region has a great significance due to its physical contiguity with Bhutan, (China) Tibet, Myanmar and Bangladesh. This region is one of the strongest source of resources.[40] It is strategically important for a number of reasons. From accessibility point of view Siliguri corridor is India's only link with this region. If China or Bangladesh or both could close the corridor at

NORTH-EAST INDIA

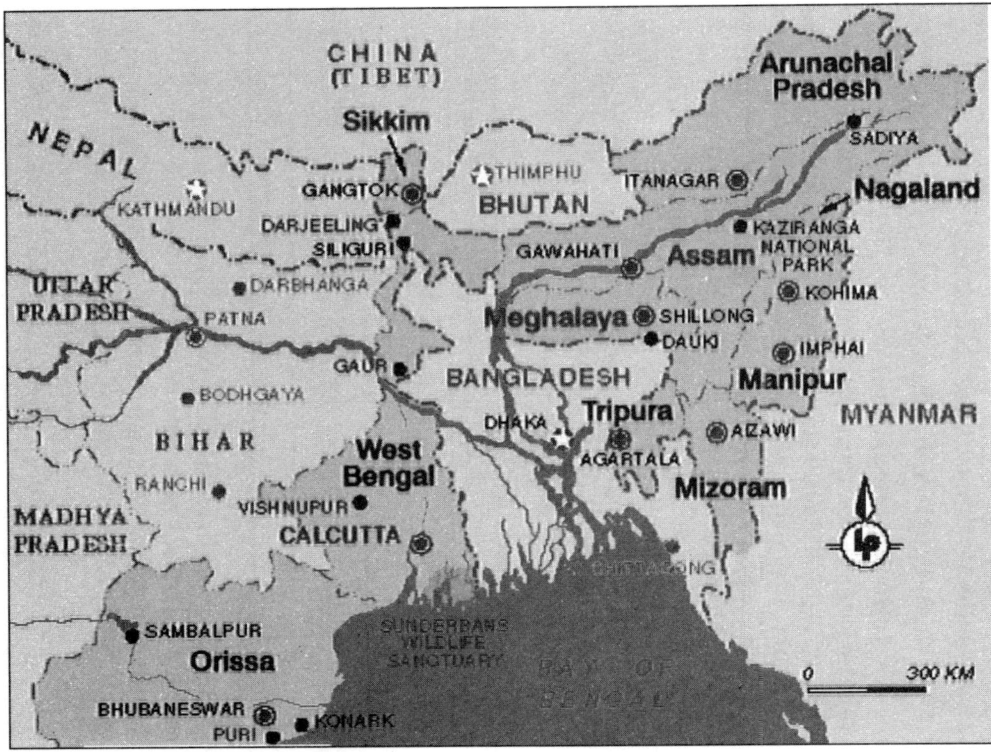

Sketch No. 9:
North East Region of India and Neighbours
Source: Internet : Google Search Engine

MAP NOT TO SCALE

will, there is no answer to this visible threat, it would cut off the rest of the region from India. The total width of this Siliguri corridor is 30 km only. [41]

India's north-east land boundary is complicated and poses numbers of socio-cultural, historical, traditional and security problems. India's north-east boundary is totally different from northern and western land boundary of India. The study of this boundary would be carried out into two parts.

A) Indo-Myanmar (Outer boundary)

B) Indo-Bangladesh (Inner boundary)

A) Indo-Myanmar Boundary:- The Indo-Myanmar boundary is one of the critical boundaries which poses a number of socio-cultural and maintenance problems. This boundary has proximity with four north-eastern states Mizoram, Manipur, Nagaland and Arunachal Pradesh by having a length of 1643 km. This is a natural boundary, accepted and confirmed by both the countries of India and Myanmar. This boundary line passes through dense forest and altitudes with the Mizo hills, Manipur and Nagaland on the Indian side and on the Myanmar side through China Hills, Naga Hills and Kachin state. [42]

Name of Indian State/Area	District adjoining Myanmar
Arunachal Pradesh	Lu, Khonsa Tapur
Mizoram	Vanlaiphai
Manipur	Chmachandpur, Palel, Imphal, Ukhrol and Maozore Zang
Nagaland	Kohima, Mokokenugn Mon

The population of this border area basically and in majority is tribal. In addition to the tribal population, the Hindu, Muslim and Bengali population also exist. The tribal people of this area have an ethnic connection with the Shan tribes of Myanmar since pre-British period. Accessibility is poor, it is very difficult to construct road or bridge specially in border area. To have an access to northern Myanmar, the 'Ledo Road' is available. Even through Kohima and Imphal also it is accessible. Japanese had access through Kohima-Imphal during World War II.

The Indo-Myanmar boundary is a natural one and basically it was finalised in A.D 1401 as a result of Ahoms, Rulers of Assam, and Burmese war. The crest of Patkoi mountain ranges was finalised as the Indo-Burmese (Myanmar) boundary. From 1401, time to time this traditional and natural boundary was confirmed by the contemporary rulers—treaty of Yendaboo 1926, 1967—and in 1976 joint boundary commission of India and Myanmar conducted 18th meeting and confirmed it. From security point of view this boundary is more difficult than the western boundary; this boundary passes through high altitudes and dense forest. Lack of feelings of nationalism among the tribes on either side belonging to same ethnic stock, as well as heavy rainfall pose a number of problems for the maintenance of the border area. [43] The cordial relationship between Chinese and Military dictator of Myanmar and the growing presence of Chinese in Northern Myanmar tract i.e. Indo-Myanmar border area, has a great concern for the security of India.

B) Indo-Bangladesh Boundary: After leaving the outer boundary of India with Myanmar, the inner one lies along with Bangladesh. This boundary was determined by Bengal Boundary Commission at the time of partition. This commission was chaired by Sir Cyril Radcliff and assisted by two Hindu justices Mr. B.K. Mukherjee and Mr. C.C. Biswas and two Muslim justices A.S. Mohammed Akram and S.A. Rahman. Like Indo-Pak western land boundary, this Indo-Bangladesh boundary (previously East Pakistan) poses a number of problems. This commission has left a lot of discrepancies. [44] This boundary passes through west Bengal, Assam, Meghalaya, Tripura and Mizoram.

Sr.No.	Indian State Physical Contiguity with Indo-Bangladesh boundary	Border area / District
1.	West Bengal	Koch Bihar, Jal Paiguri, Balurghat, Beharampur, Krishnanagar, Barasat.
2.	Assam	Karimganj, Dullabchara, Golapara, Dhubri
3.	Meghalaya	Willian Nagar, Tura, Mawsynram, Cherrapunji, Dauki
4.	Tripura	Radhakishorpur, Agartala, Amarpur, Belonia, Sonamura, Kailash, Anar
5.	Mizoram	Saiha, Demagin, Langlei

It has the length of 4,351 kilometers. The war between India and Pakistan in 1971 introduced geopolitical changes in South Asia with the creation of Bangladesh. This boundary presents varieties of terrain, plain, flat, deep valleys, riverine, hilly jungle; on account of paddy land during monsoon it is used to get flooded.

The population comprises a variety of religion-culture; Hindus, Muslims, Bengalis and Christians, even tribals. This boundary line separates the two countries despite the similar ethnic, religious, linguistic and cultural character on both sides. [45]

The problem of habitation of the border belt of Indo-Bangladesh is a major one. The density of population on Indo-Bangladesh border varies from state to state. In some of the sectors the border area is heavily populated and cultivation is carried out till the end of border.

The military geography also poses a number of security problems. Transportation and communication can be managed in maximum sectors but erecting the permanent border outpost in some of the areas is difficult, due to swelling of the water of Brahmaputra and other rivers which increase the depth of the river by 20 to 30 feets. Patrolling in such areas is another headache. To check and pursue the infiltrators, smugglers, illegal migrants, trade and traffic is a serious challenge to the security forces. Increasing role of I.S.I of Pakistan and insurgents and terrorist camps in Bangladesh poses a great concern for India's security. [46]

The delimitation of Indo-Pak (Eastern-Pakistan) boundary determined by Bengal Boundary Commission has left a number of ambiguities and loopholes. To deal with all discrepancies and sort out the problems relevant to Indo-Bangladesh border, the Indo-Bangladesh agreement was signed in 1974. But after the death of Sheikh Mujibur Rehman, this agreement could not solve the purpose. Except Sheikh Hassina Wajed, every Government of Bangladesh adopted anti-Indian stand and worked against Indian interest. The enclaves and non-demarcated boundary poses practical problems. Despite spending more than 35 years, both the countries are yet to sort out the "Problem of Demarcation". There is about acres of area with Bangladesh which is non-demarcated (Daighata, West Bengal Muhuri river, Tripura and Lalthitilla-Dumabari Assam). Non-demarcated area of this boundary has remained a source of tension and minor skirmishes between Border Security Force of India and Bangladesh Rifles. Even today India has yet to construct the roads and fencing of this boundary, at present 1000 km (approx) boundary remains incomplete. Increasing influence of the Chinese, I.S.I of Pakistan in Bangladesh has a great challenge and at the same time immigration from Bangladesh to the Indian states specially north-east states created the problem of "Identical Crises" for local population.[47] The constant flow of this foreign influx from Bangladesh—not only north-east states but various parts of India—has been a major concern and this is to be sorted out at diplomatic level as well as various measures in border area.

11.2 Geostrategic Importance of India's Maritime Boundaries

11.2.1 Historical Account:

The subject "Maritime Boundaries" has never been paid due attention in India except during ancient time. It was the Cholas, Pallvas, Maurya, Gupta who were vigilant about maritime security but afterward the Indian rulers did not consider the significance of sea frontiers. And as a result of it, they had paid heavy price i.e. invasion, sack and raid by foreigners—Mohammad Gazni, Ghori, Mohammed bin Kasim, who invaded this country through land borders. And then the Dutch, French, Portuguese and finally the British had established their colonies and India became one of the parts of British Empire. [48] Admiral A.T. Mahan rightly said, "Negligence towards sea frontiers would be the subject of mercy by other nations. Therefore, it is highly essential that rulers of the country must pay due attention towards the security of Maritime Boundaries."

The security of maritime boundaries is in many ways different rather than land borders. The oceans spread over millions of kilometers away and it's very difficult to pin-point the enemy's presence whether it is within our maritime boundary or outside. Thus the reason for such ambiguity is inaccurate. It's very difficult to set an identification mark in ocean or high seas, like we could set variety of identification marks on the land boundaries—barbed fencing, pillar, vistas, wall etc. In view of these complications, it must be acknowledged that maintenance of security and sovereignty of "Maritime Boundaries" has been a challenging task.

11.2.2 India's Maritime Boundaries and Indian Ocean: (sketch no.10)

India has a vast coastline both on the west and east. The total length of the sea coast is 5600 kilometers (approx) which is the longest amongst the littoral countries of Indian Ocean. The eastern arm is Bay of Bengal Sea while western arm is Arabian Sea. [49]

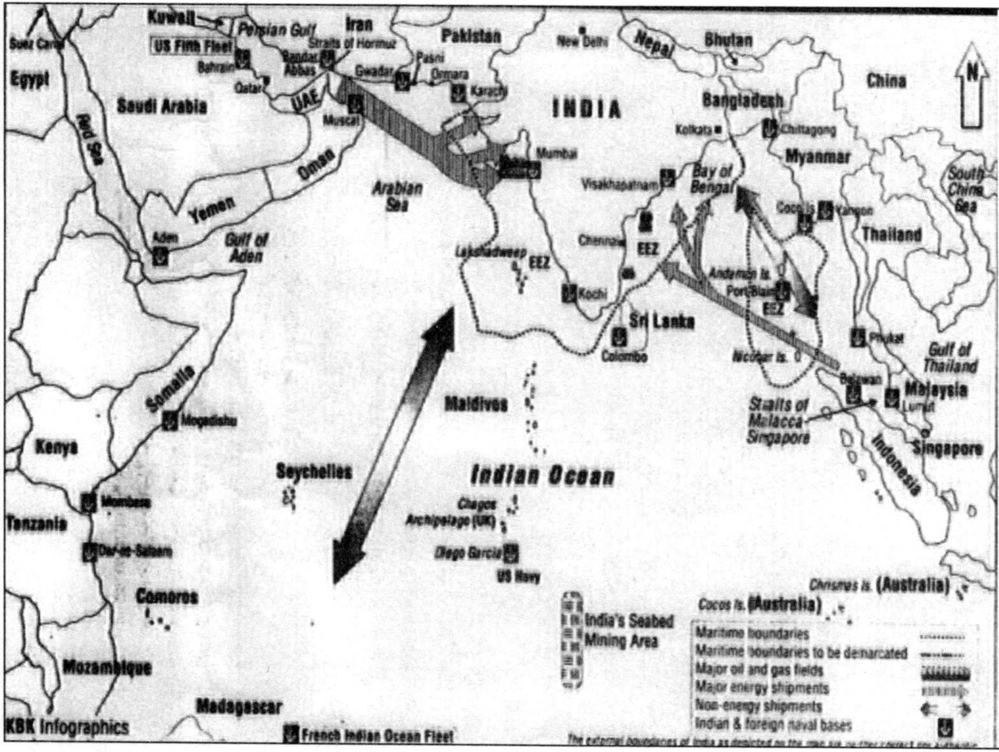

INDIA'S MARITIME SECURITY

Sketch No. 10:
Diego Garcia, Andaman, Nicobar and Lakshdeweep. India's Maritime Boundaries.

Source: Rahul Roy Chaudhury "India's Maritime Security", Knowledge World Publications, New Delhi, 2000.

MAP NOT TO SCALE

According to the "Laws of the sea" India has the following limits of Maritime boundaries.

Sr.No.	Nature of Boundaries	**Distance** in nautical miles (from baselines)
1.	Territorial water/sea	12
2.	Contiguous sea	24
3.	Continental sea	200
4.	Exclusive Economic Sone	200

Sources: Proceedings of National Congress for Defence Studies, XVI, University of Allahabad, 2005, p-135.

Indian Ocean is one of the largest oceans and covers an area of 74 million sq. km. The Indian Ocean holds 65% of strategic raw materials, natural gas 30% and comprises 30% of world population. In this region gold, uranium and diamonds are found and even possibilities of discovery of the variety of minerals from seabed. India is one of the largest littoral countries having the oldest civilization. The title of this ocean itself indicates the close proximity with India. The Indian culture is well-known and proliferated in this sphere of Indian Ocean. [50] In pursuit of her maritime security India is putting every effort to pass the resolution on Indian Ocean as a zone of peace and make it free from the nuclearisation and militarisation.

The, Ist World War was fought in the Atlantic Ocean mainly, then Second World War took place in Pacific Ocean and Mediterranean sea. But if the third world war takes place then definitely it will be in the Indian Ocean. This prediction is based on the ground reality i.e. super power's rivalry in Indian Ocean (even after disintegration of USSR). Being the largest littoral country of Indian Ocean, "India's maritime security" has been challenged by this strategic environment in the Indian Ocean. India's maritime boundaries have close proximity with Indian Ocean. The

Indian Peninsula divides the northern periphery of the Indian Ocean in the east as the Bay of Bengal and in the west Arabian Sea. In view of this material fact maritime boundary of India acquires more strategic significance as never before.

11.2.3 Scope and Significance

India's Bay of Bengal is the fulcrum between the Malacca strait and Gulf of Hormiz. It is a junction and comprises important sea lanes for trade and commerce.[51] The well-known islands of Andaman & Nicobar are scattered into 572 pieces on this eastern flank. This eastern flank is very rich in terms of resources. According to Geological Survey of India the vast gas reserve—hydrocarbon reserve in the Krishna-Godavari basin of Andhra Pradesh is available. And untapped fish stocks and seabed minerals itself gives evidence that India's maritime boundaries have immense wealth. One third of the world's trade and almost all of East Asian countries oil supply pass through this eastern strait.

India's western flank, Arabian Sea, is an open sea which dominates India's sea lanes to Europe, Russia, America, Africa and West Asia. Approximately 70% of oil India is importing via sea lanes from the West Asia. This western arms of India includes Lakshadweep Islands which can provide air-cover and naval protection during emergency. By virtue of this, it is possible to project land- based air power over this area. The well-known Bombay now Mumbai High is a source of energy of oil and the natural gas is also situated in this area.

India conducting her foreign trade around 97% in volume is sea borne. And 98% of oil supply India receives is by sea transportation. India's sea borne trade is growing very rapidly and the simple reason is trade through sea lanes would be cheap than air or other transportation. It proves that Indian Ocean has been of distinct strategic and economic value for India. It would be feasible to say that India's destiny is highly dependent on the Indian Ocean for its prosperity, security and development.

11.2.4 India's Maritime Security and Interest

Number of super powers directly and indirectly are projecting their presence in Indian Ocean. The policies, programme and strategic behaviours of the "Powers" including China and Pakistan, has a great concern to India's maritime security. In view of this, Government of India also adopted a number of measures to defend our interest as well as security of the country. The Naval Budget is being increased from time to time and due attention is paid to strengthen the maritime security. To counter Pakistani's acquisition of "Agosta" from France, Government of India acquired scorpion submarine. The tri-service command also has been established on Andaman and Nicobar Islands. In order to improve maritime surveillance in A.D. 2002 India has acquired UAV. i.e. Unmanned Aerial Vehicles. In addition to that full many a number of changes is being introduced in Indian Navy such as, Hydrographic Department. Even early warning system regarding Tsunami also was designed to introduce at the earliest. [53] In view of the strategic milieu in Indian Ocean and to preserve the security and interest of the country, India must opt for the following steps:

1. Safeguard the passage with "Freedom" in high seas.
2. Protect economic interest and exploit maritime resources.
3. Check the illegal entry or attempt of tapping the water minerals. And act as checkers for thwarting of arms and drugs into Indian territory.

In view of the above task, Indian maritime forces must be vigilant and perform this assignment effectively.

11.2.5 India's Maritime Strategy

As regards to India's maritime security challenges and interest of the country, India's maritime strategy is to be considered as follows:

1. Basically, India is the largest littoral country on the Indian Ocean having fifth largest Naval power with minimum nuclear credible deterrence; but our policy is based on

humanity, peace and development.[54] And hence, our policy regarding Indian Ocean is to use it for economic development, "live and let live" based on the welfare of human being.

2. India do not want to present any outsider in power in this region and therefore carrying out her diplomatic pursuit at diplomatic level to pass the resolution i.e. "Indian ocean as a zone of Peace" and free from nuclearisation by any means.[55]
3. For administrative support and efficiency, the present facilities and infrastructure should be expanded like repairing, refuelling, bunkering, post dockyard, communication, radar, early warning system against enemy, natural calamities etc.
4. In order to exploit untapped water minerals and resources, India must develop her infrastructural facilities like fishing harbour with cold storage, food processing industries, radio communication, navigation, radar etc.[56] It is to be mentioned that there were wider scopes to enhance expertise in the tapping of resources.
5. Since the Independence of the country in 1947, adequate attention was not paid towards naval preparedness. From 1971 experience we have learnt a lot and as a result, Naval Budget has been increased from time to time. But in view of the scenario in Indian Ocean and planning and programmes of our adversaries, India has to pay maximum attention and emphasis on naval preparedness. The modernisation programs of Navy and sub Naval forces have to be expedited and ensured that "Maritime Forces" should be capable of performing their responsibilities with result-oriented programme.

Footnotes

1. B.L. Sukhwal, *Modern Political Geography of India,* Sterling Publication, Jalandhar, 1985, India, p.1.

2. Lt.Col. M.G. Abhyankar, Retd., *Defence Principles and Organisation*, Usha Prakashan, Ganeshkhand, India, Pune 1974, p.19.
3. N. S. Jamwal, Management of Land Border, *Strategic Analysis*, Vol. 26, No.3, July-Sept 2002, Institute for Defence Studies and Analysis, old JNU Campus, New Delhi, p.409.
4. Lt.Col.M.G. Abhyankar, Retd., *op. cit.*, p.21.
5. R.L.Singh, India: A Regional Geography, National Geographical Society of India, Varanasi, 1998, pp. 80-84.
6. Lt.Col M.G. Abhyankar, Retd., *op. cit.*, p.32.
7. *Ibid.*, p.31.
8. R.L. Singh, *op. cit.*, pp. 54-58.
9. Lt. Col. M.G. Abhyankar, Retd, *op. cit.*, p.31.
10. *Ibid.*, p.30.
11. R.L. Singh, *op. cit.*, pp. 348-352.
12. Lt.Col. M.G. Abhyankar, Retd, *op.cit.*, p.29.
13. B.L. Sukhwal, *India: A Political Geography*, Allied Publishers Bombay, 1971, p.194.
14. Rajendra Prasad, "Sino-Indian Border Dispute", Seminar paper, Deptt. of Defence and Strategic Studies, University of Gorakhpur, November 1984.
15. Government of India, *The Sino-Indian Border Dispute, Question and Answer*, Ministry of Information and Broadcasting Publication Division, 1963, New Delhi, pp.23-24.
16. B.L. Sukhwal, 1971, *op. cit.*, pp. 210-14.
17. Dr. P.C. Dutta, *Arunachal Pradesh: An Overview*, Directorate of Research, Government of Arunachal Pradesh, Itanagar, 1993, p.56.
18. Madhok V.K., *The Para Military Forces: Need for Merger and Reorganisation: In Repowering National Security*, Aditya Prakashan, 1998, Mumbai, p.20.
19. Gp. Capt. S.G. Chitnis, Retd., *India's Defence Expenditure: An Examination*, Department of Defence and Strategic Studies, University of Pune, Oct 1985, Pune, India.
20. Satish Kumar, Ed., *Year book on India's Foreign Policy 1985-86*, Sage Publications, New Delhi, 1988, p.153.

21. B.L. Sukhwal, *India: A Political Geography,* Allied Publisher, Bombay, 1971, pp. 206-07.
22. Sahadev Vohra, "Parameters of a Border Settlement with China", *Mainstream,* March-31, Vol. XXVIII, No.23, New Delhi, pp.16-18.
23. C.S. Bose, *Geography of The Himalaya,* National Book Trust India, 1972, pp. 32-36.
24. Muthib, *A Social and Economic Atlas of India,* Delhi, Oxford University Press, 1987, pp. 94-95.
25. O.P. Singh, *The Himalaya:Nature, Man and Culture,* Rajesh Publication, New Delhi, 1983, p.234.
26. Government of India, *The Sino-Indian Boundary Text of Treaties, Agreement and Certain Exchange of Notes Relating to The Sino-Indian Boundary,* The Indian Society of International Law, Parliament Street, New Delhi-1, 1962, pp.110-11.
27. C.S. Bose, *op. cit.,* p. 153.
28. N.S. Jamwal, *op. cit., Strategic Analysis,* Vol.26, No.3, July-Sept 2003, p..419.
29. C.S. Bose, *op. cit.,* p.173-75.
30. Surya P. Sharma, *India's Boundary and Territorial Dispute,* Vikas Publication, New Delhi; 1971, p. 13.
31. B. L. Suhkwal, *op.cit.,* 1971, pp. 203-04.
32. Sudhakar Bhat, *India and China,* Popular Book Service, New Delhi, 1967, pp.57-58.
33. Sahadev Vohra, "Sinkiang and Ladakh", *USI Journal,* New Delhi, 1990, Sept; pp.115-17.
34. P.C. Chakravarti, *India-China Relations,* Mukhopadhyay Publishers, Calcutta, 1961, p.146.
35. Sudhakar Bhat, *op. cit.,* p.49.
36. Tejvir Singh and Jagdish Kaur, *Studies in Economic Development: Himalayan Mountain and Men,* Print House, Lucknow, 1983 p.20.
37. Major Sitaram Johri, Retd., *Chinese Invasion of NEFA,* Himalayan Publication, Lucknow, India, 1968, pp..18-19.
38. *The Times of India,* New Delhi, 29th Jan 1993.

39. Lt. Col. M.G. Abhyankar, Retd., *op. cit.*, p.25.
40. O.P. Khanna, "North-East Region Security Challenges. *The Competition Master*, Vol. XXVIII, No.12, July, 1987, Industrial Area, Chandigarh, India, 1987, pp.882-84.
41. Balkrishnan Nair, *Facts of Indian Defence*, S. Chand and Co., Ramnagar, New Delhi, 1985, pp.56-57.
42. Government of India, "White Paper No. I," Ministry of External Affairs, New Delhi, Nov. 1959, p.129.
43. R.N. Singh, "Engaging Inscrutable Myanmar", *Indian Defence Review*, Lancer Publisher, New Delhi 16, 2004, pp.51-52.
44. N.S. Jamwal, "Border Management: Dilemma of Guiding the India Bangladesh Border", *Strategic Analysis,* Vol. 28, No.1, Jan-Mar 2004, Institute for Defence Studies and Analysis, old JNU campus, New Delhi, pp.5-6.
45. B .L. Sukhwal, *Modern Political Geography of India*, Sterling Publication, Jalandhar, 1985, pp. 277-78.
46. N. S. Jamwal, *Strategic Analysis*, Vol. 28, No.1, *op. cit.*, pp. 15-18.
47. N. S. Jamwal, *Strategic Analysis*, Vol.26, No.3 , July-Sept 2002, *op. cit.*, pp. 414-16.
48. V. Tripathi and S.Pandy, "India's Maritime Challenges in 21st Century", *Proceedings of XVIth National Congress for Defence Studies*, Deptt. of Defence and Strategic Studies, University of Allahabad, 2005, p.134.
49. B.L. Sukhwal, 1971 *op. cit.*, p. 34.
50. G. S. Khurana, "Maritime Security In The Indian Ocean: Convergance Plus Co-operation Equals Resonance", *Strategic Analysis,* Vol.28, No.3, July-Sept 2004, I.D.S., Old J.N.U. Campus, New Delhi, p.413.
51. Anand Mathur, "Growing Importance of The Indian Ocean in post cold war era and its Implications for India", *Strategic Analysis*, Vol-26, No.4, Oct-Dec-2002, I.D.S. Old campus, New Delhi, p.551.
52. Gurpreet Khurana, "Co-operation Among Maritime Security Forces: Imperatives for India and Southeast Asia", *Strategic Analysis*, Vol.29, No.2, April-Jan. 2005, I.D.S. Old campus, New Delhi, p.304.

53. *Ibid.*, p.306.
54. Anand Mathur, *op. cit.*, p.553.
55. *Ibid.*, p. 551.
56. Mr.K.R. Singh, "Maritime Security: An Integrated Approach", Seminar paper 23rd and 24th Oct. 2001, School of International Studies, Jawaharlal Nehru University, New Delhi.

✣ ✣ ✣

12

TYPES OF LAND WARFARE

12.1 INTRODUCTION

Once the decision is taken by the respective 'Government' to launch a war as a last resort, then it becomes a morale binding on the Generals to ensure that this last resort should yield an expected result. The job of the Generals begins i.e. how, where and when the war to be conducted? It is not the Generals but the factors like "nature of the terrain", which will decide how, where and when the war is to be conducted. For example, the war in "Jungle" would be operated during November to April only.

Being a citizen of India and the student of defence studies, it is highly essential to have an adequate knowledge of different types of terrain and warfare. And the ultimate reason is that the Indian land borders have a variety of terrain. Starting from India's western land border which encompasses every type of terrains like Gujarat and Rajasthan has desert and sand dunes area. The Punjab sector has plain and flat area whereas the Jammu and Kashmir has dense forest including deep valleys and chains of mountains. India's Northern border has been occupied by chains of the mighty Himalayan ranges along with forest at the bottom area. The North-East border has been occupied by mountains, jungles and even some area with plain and flat terrain.

In view of the nature of terrain of India's land borders, it is vital to study the types of land warfare and have a proper understanding of the nature of various problems in jungle, high altitude, plain and desert warfare.

12.2 Plain Warfare

Plain Warfare

Characteristic of Plain Area	Tactical Problems and Feasible W&E	Logistic Problems
1. Accessibility	1. Tanks /APC	1. Maximum requirements
2. Mobility	2. Heavy Fire Weapons	2. Dumping problems
3. Observation	3. Engineer and Signal	3. Challenge to Medical Services
	4. Infantry	4. Workshop facilities
4. Bridges & Canals	5. Limitations on 'Air force'	5. Fuel for Aircrafts
5. Collection of water	6. Responsibilites ofthe Para military	

12.2.1 Characteristics of the Plain Area

1. **Accessibility:** The term "accessibility" indicates the capacity to reach upto the desired target or intended location. Normally in plain and flat area both the entities can employ the various means of transportation. On account of plain and flat area the numbers of optional roads, routes will be available. In the plain and flat terrain we can have numbers of substitute accessible options, for example, if there is no road then you can have foot tracks, railway-gauge, boat sampan etc. In plain and flat area, accessibility is very rich, in which we can have numbers of substitute ways to reach up to the desired target or location. This terrain offers extreme

accessibility as well as mobility. This might be the reason for consecutive invasion on Punjab by foreigners in the past.

2. **Mobility:** It's one of the principles of war, needless to mention that the plain and flat area is an open invitation to the exclusive use of tank. The special feature of this terrain is that it offers extreme mobility. On account of availability of numbers of road routes, tracks, railway gauge, variety of vehicles can be employed. By virtue of employment of numbers of vehicles at a time, it resulted in extreme mobility, vehicles like truck, jeep, motorcycles, two wheelers, aircrafts, helicopters, railways can move from one place to another without any difficulty or delay.

3. **Observation:** The plain and flat area has no hazard or obstruction in the battlefield. Hence there is no hazard, it means absolutely nobody will be in between fire weapons and desired target. In this plain terrain target would be located easily. An observation officer or field commander can direct exact location of the target to the gunners, soldiers or concerned in-charge. The gunner, soldier or attacker can throw the unrestricted fire without any obstruction.

4. **Bridge and Canals:** One of the features of the plain area is that you could find a number of rivers, some of them wide and may be narrow. And on account of "Green Revolution" we can see the network of canals. Hence the canals and rivers are there, and then obviously bridge will be found. These canals and rivers sometimes prove very beneficial and sometimes they become a great headache. During war, as a part of sabotage or terrorist activities, the bridge may be a subject of bomb-blast. In such a case a bridge becomes a sort of disadvantage to its holder. [1]

5. **Water Collection:** Collection of water is hazardous in the plain area. This can be found in stable or variable forms. As a part of the stable water collection, Pakistan has constructed "Ichogil canal" near the city of Lahore.

This canal was deliberately constructed by Pakistan in order to forbid the Indian troops movement from Punjab sector of India. The unexpected rainfall also can be an obstacle or check the movements of vehicles and especially tanks. During Indo-Pak war of 1965 in Khemkaran sector, the Pakistani tanks got stuck. It happened due to "water collection" only which was managed by the Indian Army. [2] The canal water was spilled over to the area where the Pakistani Army had a dream to trap and beat the Indian force.

12.2.2 Tactical Problems and Feasible Weapons and Equipments

The overall characteristic of the plain area indicates that the warfare in this flat terrain is against the safety and security of the soldiers. In plain area, on the other hand, there is obstruction in the movements of the combat forces easily watched by the enemy. On account of accessibility and probability, "unrestricted fire" becomes unavoidable in such circumstances and for this soldiers have to pay very heavy price. In view of this "risk" security of life, specific weapons and equipments are suitable in this plain and flat area.

1. **Tanks :** Plain and flat terrain is most suitable for tanks to carry out the tactical manoeuvre. By virtue of railway gauge network, it can be carried out by trains upto the desired point. The tank is the weapon which provides "security" upto certain extent. The Punjab sector of Indo-Pak border is feasible for "Tank Warfare".
2. **Heavy Fire Weapons:** On account of plain and flat area, the heavy artillery guns, machine guns, mortars can be employed on a large scale. It is possible only in plain area in which such heavy fire weapons can be carried out from one place to another. This is an area where you can "concentrate" your fire power easily.

3. **Engineers and Signals:** In modern warfare the technocrats have numbers of responsibilities on the battlefield. The modern war is fought by the brain of technocrats, in plain warfare they are supposed to do numbers of jobs such as supporting our combat forces and so on. To clear the mines which are spread by our enemy on the route of advance to contact. In the same capacity spread-up of the mines is to be done on the possible route of the enemy. If the bridge is destroyed by the enemy, the substitute arrangement has to be made by us.[3]

   As plain warfare has extreme "Mobility", it becomes very difficult to maintain the communication and coordination within the various branches of combat forces. So it is the primary responsibility of Signal to provide the sophisticated telephones, wireless, mobile instrument and infrastructure in order to maintain the inter communication within the various branches of combat forces. And at the same time they must put their efforts to catch/tap the intercommunication of enemy's troops.

4. **Infantry:** Infantry is rightly called the "Queen" of battle. It is the Infantry who are supposed to open-up the major fury with enemy. In plain warfare only an Infantry can attend extreme mobility. This can be attended by variety of vehicles. In view of the nature of plains warfare it is highly essential to deploy maximum infantry troops.[4] An Infantry has numbers of merits along with special feature i.e. tactical manoeuvre which is vital in plain warfare.

5. **Limitations on "Air Force":** In plain warfare an "Air Force" has a great significance as well as limitations. On the plain ground there are no obstructions. Despite it, airpower cannot perform her role of air reconnaissance and photography. By virtue of plain

and flat terrain the aircraft/helicopter can be shot down by enemy's anti-aircraft gun. In plain warfare camouflage and concealment are almost impossible and therefore an observation is possible by the air force. Over and above, the significant role of air force cannot be denied, despite some limitation. Air power can provide close support to Infantry during assault by tactical bombing wherever it is required.[5]

6. **Responsibilities of Para Military Troops:** The Plain warfare is extremely mobile, offensive and verily a destructive war. The combat forces have numbers of responsibilities and hence the protection of airfield, strips, important bridges, installations would be managed by the Para Military troops. [6] In addition to these troops for air borne operation and unit of anti-aircraft gun must be vigilant to tackle any situation at any moment.

12.2.3 Logistics Problems

1. **More and Maximum Requirements:** It is considered that warfare in plains will have extreme mobility. It is assumed that soldiers and vehicles will advance with greater speed and obviously maximum ration, ammunition and fuel will be required.
2. **Dumping Problems:** War in the plains having extreme mobility requires more and more food, fuel, ammunitions. In order to procure maximum requirements of the combat forces, it is highly essential to dump and maintain the stockpiles of all the required goods and commodities at every point and level. It is a genuine problem that during war-skirmishes how the safety, security and secrecy about stocks at every front would be maintained. There are chances of bombing by the enemy sometimes deliberately or unknowingly.
3. **Challenges to Medical Services:** By virtue of mobility and rapid movements of combat forces the

ratio of casualties will be more. As compared to other warfare, the war in the plains is more horrible and destructive. We can find the maximum numbers of wounded soldiers. So the wounded soldiers must be given medical relief without any further delay. Candidly, it's a challenge to medical services to cope-up with the situation and save the human life with available resources.

4. **Workshop Facilities:** In view of the extreme mobility of plains warfare, it is to be understood that when the vehicles, tanks, firearms work with more rapidity, they may need servicing and repairing. To meet these specific requirements, it is vital that workshop facilities should be made available with adequate infrastructure. An attempt should be made to get repaired or servicing the tanks, vehicles or weapons within the stipulated time. [7] In addition to this, major repairing facilities also should be made available. Sincere and serious efforts should be made that how every vehicle, weapon or tank will rejoin or be reused for the battle.

5. **Fuel for Aircrafts:** Needless to mention that after World War II, the "Air Force" is being recognized as a dominant force and key to attain the victory during war. The air power has a determinant role, whatever may be the warfare. It is to be remembered that each and every movement of aircraft depends upon fuel. Purified petrol known as "Aviation Fuel"[8] is required for aircrafts, helicopters and choppers.

Maintenance and dumping of vast aviation fuel is a costly affairs. Taking into consideration the exclusive role of air power during every type of warfares, the aviation fuel is required in a large quantity.

12.2 Desert Warfare

Desert Warfare

Characteristic	Tactical Problems	Logistic Problems
1. Scarcity of water	1. Infantry	1. Storage of water
2. Difficult "Nature"	2. Tanks and APC	2. Storage of fuel
3. Poor accessibility	3. Camel Force	3. Camouflage and concealment
	4. Water source of confrontation	4. Requirements of construction material
	5. Limited roads	5. Medical Relief and Workshop Facilities.
	6. Difficulties during advance	
	7. Night operations only	
	8. Use of Air Power	

12.3.1 Characteristic of Desert

The Rajasthan sector of Indo-Pak border has desert belt adjoining Ganganagar, Barmer, Bikaner and Jaisalmer districts. Therefore, we must have adequate knowledge of the characteristics, tactical, and logistics problems in desert area.

1. **Scarcity of water:** In the desert, water is a precious commodity. It is truly said that in desert blood is cheap but water is costly. Scarcity of water in the desert is a genuine problem. There you will find the sand, dust, and heat. Lack of water is an acute problem. In the desert belt, within 30 to 40 km you can find water-well which has a depth of 300 to 400 feet.
2. **Difficult "Nature":** Desert area by nature is very rough and tough which offers a number of challenges for human tolerance during "day." One would find the temperature very high and uncomfortable and absolutely a contrast during night i.e. weather at night becomes very cool. "Wind" has negative implications; it blows consecutively

which creates dunes i.e. sand hills. These sand dunes prove hazardous for the movements of human beings. Really the survival in such a critical condition is a hard test of tolerance capacity for the soldiers.

3. **Poor Accessibility:** Nature is against development; due to critical circumstances one cannot find so many roads or substitute roads, route or tracks in this terrain. Roads are limited and hence accessibility gets hampered in this "Desert Warfare". Construction of road is a very costly affair. In this area you would find that population is sparse and scattered and every village has limited population.[9] As in plain area you cannot find rich accessibility in the desert area. Accessibility is poor and restricted by sand dunes. Vehicles or men should not go off the proper road unknowingly, if so, they can get stuck in the sand.

12.3.2 Tactical Problems

Except few basic differences, the tactical problems of combat forces seems to be similar to the plain warfare. The warfare in desert also has extreme "Mobility". In desert warfare, there are still a number of problems like transportation, limitations of air power etc.

1. **Infantry:** Infantry is not only a queen of battle but also a backbone of a combat force. Without active involvement by Infantry, the war on the ground has no meaning. Infantry has a capacity to cover a distance of 30 to 40 kilometers per day.[10] Physically rough and tough soldiers are the assets of this kind of warfare.

2. **APC and Tank:** APC i.e. Armored Personnel Carriers are like mini tanks. APC appear like boxes with no roofs. Approximately 25 to 30 soldiers can ride it. By virtue of track, it can work like a mini-tank. Tank is the chief weapon as well as a vehicle in desert warfare. Tank is the weapon which provides "firepower, mobility, and security and transportation facilities". Due to horse power of tank's engine, sand-dunes cannot stop them. During North African campaign of World War II, tank

had played a determinant role. Though tank is the basic weapon of desert warfare, we must be aware of the limitations on the "use of tank".[11] Tank can be a subject of serious threat from land mines, air strike and anti tank weapon, like RCL gun etc.

3. **Camel Force:** Camel is the animal which has certain features. It is considered more useful in desert. Camel can walk 60 to 80 km distance within a day with minimum food and water. Without water for a longer period it can work, walk and survive in desert area. By virtue of the utility of this animal, it is rightly called the "ship of the desert". This might be the reason therefore, that the invaders of India, in the past Arabs, Turks, Sultan etc. had "camel force". Even today, for combat purpose camel can be used for observation, patrolling and assault purpose in desert warfare.

4. **"Water" Source of Confrontation:** Water is a precious commodity. Without it the survival of human being is highly impossible. In desert, "water" has its own significance and becomes more costly than blood. In desert the water point or well, becomes a backbone of hostility and fighting goes on between the two enemies for hours and hours just to capture the water point or well. So in desert warfare especially the water point or well becomes a source of conflict.

5. **Limited Roads**: In order to carry out the movements of combat forces in desert, the roads are limited. Construction of road is very difficult. Though it is constructed, it may get stuck in the sand-dunes.[12]

6. **Difficulties During Advance:** During advance the maintenance of "secrecy" becomes a difficult task. While passing through the sand, the foot prints are visible and it can be traced out easily by enemy's aircraft which is conducting reconnaissance. During advance to contact the enemy, if any soldier stops just for relaxing or tying the shoe anklet or for any other reason, it becomes very difficult for him to rejoin his comrade or group. And

once he misses even it becomes very problematic to find out the direction whether it is North, South or East.

7. **Night Operations Only:** In desert warfare we can find extreme heat, dust and temperature, which is unbearable for human beings. In such a critical circumstance conducting any operation is not so feasible. It is not so advisable to concentrate and employ the fire weapons during extreme temperature, heat and dust. [13] In view of such circumstances, the field commanders normally prefer to carry out their operation during night only.
8. **Use of Air Power:** The airpower has definitely a determinant role during desert warfare. The overall battle zone can be a subject of reconnaissance, photography and even air strike. The relevant officers have to ensure that their aircraft does not become the subject of anti-aircraft gun by the enemy. Air power can provide a close and result-oriented support to ground forces. [14] The battle of Longanwala during Indo-Pak war of 1971 is a distinct example in this context. The Indian Air Force had played a very crucial role in order to destroy the Pakistani tanks in this battle and proved that air power can provide an active support to the ground forces.

12.3.3 Logistic Problems

As a part of' normalcy, the logistic problems in desert area will be similar to those in the plain area, except some of the special needs of the combat forces.

1. **Storage of Water:** Additional and special requirement or problem of the desert area is "storage of water". The maintenance of "security and secrecy" of water storage is a more critical job of the logistic management in the desert. It has to be stored in the largest tank and to maintain its safety, security and secrecy, it has to be kept underground. In water-wells you can find salty water which is not so feasible for drinking purpose: if you wish to use it for drinking, then the process of desalination has to be done. Without the process of desalination one will not be able to drink such water.

2. **Storage of Fuel:** In this warfare maximum fuel is required for Tanks and Armed Personnel Carriers which plays a determinant role during war and needless to say that the tanks and A.P.C.s both require maximum fuel. It can be remembered that tanks and A.P.C.s are the soul of military operation, as without, it is not so easy to carry out the movements of combat forces in desert area. Therefore, logistic management has to maintain the stock pile of fuel in a large quantity at various fronts. And again it carries a question mark about its secrecy, security and safety.
3. **Camouflage and Concealment:** Basically it's a tactical part but logistic management has to ensure that whatever clothing, equipments, weapons, goods and commodities are supposed to be issued; they have to match the colour of sand and the surrounding environment. An attempt should be made that colour of vehicles has to be mingled up with the environment.
4. **Requirements of Construction Material:** On the soil of desert area the preparation of trench or bunker or wall is a critical task. But for "defence" purpose it has to be done. To defend ourself it is vital to prepare trenches, bunkers, and walls and therefore the construction materials like cement, bricks, steel, planks, and poles are required. So to procure the required building material is one of the major tasks of the logistics department.
5. **Medical Relief and Workshop Facilities:** In the desert area there are possibilities of different diseases and health problems for soldiers like sun or heat stroke, severe temperature, snakes or scorpions bite. In addition to this, the medical relief for wounded soldiers has to be procured without delay. So medical relief centers are to be prepared accordingly. And synonymously workshop facilities with full required infrastructure for vehicles, weapons and equipments for repairing should be made available. Attempt should be made that how these vehicles, weapons, instruments or equipments will be reused for battle. [15]

12.4 Jungle Warfare

Jungle Warfare

Characteristic	Tactical Problems	Logistic Problems
1. Nature of Jungle	1. Restricted visibility	1. Transportation
2. Ideal period for warfare	2. Restricted largest force and vehicles	2. Medical facilities
3. Water—an obstacle	3. Safety and security of Soldiers	3. Problems of construction material
4. Problematic for health	4. Challenges to Engineers	4. Need for careful planning
	5. Problems for inter-communication	5. General requirements of forces
	6. Problems for concentration of fire power	
	7. Challenges to Air power	

Preamble: The Armed Forces of India are very much familiar with jungle warfare. It may be new to the armed forces of other countries, but Indians are having an experience of this from the ancient period to onwards. Even today the Indian Army carries out their hot pursuit against insurgents and terrorists in the jungles of Northeast States and Kashmir. The Indian Army has vast experience and deep knowledge of jungle warfare since the decade of eighties, and it has been acknowledged even by U.S.A. It is the Indian Army that has trained the Army of the U.S., how to tackle with insurgents or terrorist in jungle area.

Historical Evaluation

India is a great country with her great tradition of "good warriors" having an experience of types of warfare. The term jungle warfare might be new and unknown to the world till World War II. But India is an exceptional one—the Indians are familiar with jungle warfare since the ancient time. References are being available which shows that India had adequate knowledge of jungle warfare. During ancient period Lord Rama had fought a war with the Devils to protect the Ashram of Vishwamitra in the dense forest. Kautilya had explained the philosophy of war in his book entitled "*Kautilya's Arthsastra*". Further Kautilya had focused on "types and terrain of warfare" in which jungle warfare is mentioned. In the 17th century Shivaji had fought a number of wars with his enemy in the dense forest area; for example, battle of Jawali, battle of Pratapgadh etc. The British Indian Forces, during World War II fought the war against the Japanese in jungles. [16] Even today India's land borders have an area of dense forest and hence the study of jungle warfare is vital for every Indian.

12.4.1 Characteristics

Jungle warfare is a different type of warfare with special types of features, strategy and tactics.

1. **Nature of Jungle:** There are two types of jungles—primary and secondary. Primary jungle means jungles in which man would not be able to see anything, as visibility is restricted. In such a jungle you may not find sunlight easily and would realise the existence of wild animals. In primary jungle safety, security of man may be challenged by wild animals but it can have access with certain precautionary measures. But on account of deforestation, rarely you can find such primary jungles. Another type of jungle is secondary in which you can find habitation of human beings. The activities of forest department and existence of tribals can easily be seen in this type of jungle.[17] By virtue of duties and responsibilities of forest department though it is limited, one can find some of the roads and footpaths up to a certain extent.
2. **Ideal Period for Warfare:** Normally the jungles receive heavy rainfall. During monsoon particularly in India i.e. from June to end of September and even sometimes first week of October, no warfare or warlike activities are

expected. The suitable or ideal period for jungle warfare is October to April.

This may be one of the reasons the Indo-Pak war of 1971 on the "eastern front" took place in December only. The eastern front was a "decisive" one and with a jungle area.

3. **Water an Obstacle:** As in 'desert warfare' lack of water is an acute problem, it is the same case with jungle warfare; but in jungle one can find a contrast picture i.e. lot of water itself is a problem. In jungle there are number of rivers, sub rivers, streams which really proves obstacles in smooth conduct of war in jungles. To cross such rivers, streams, the sampans and even elephants are the best that can solve the purpose easily. This jungle water is not purified and feasible for drinking purpose. But it seems to be very clean and one cannot control oneself and if one do so, then one could be subject to stomach pains, diarrhea or in some cases dysentery also. Basically, the jungles are not feasible for habitation of human beings; it is for animals and various other creatures. Heavy rainfall, extreme heat and existence of wild animals are problematic for human beings. In the jungles you can find a number of creatures—animals snakes, leeches, scorpions, reptiles etc. which pose a threat to the well-being of soldier. On account of the above facts the jungle is considered a home for many diseases like flew, malaria, severe temperature—cold, snake-bite etc.

12.4.2 Tactical Problems

1. **Restricted Visibility:** In a jungle, everywhere one would find greenery and in such greenery it is very difficult to identify an enemy who is seating close from your position. To acquire maximum results from camouflage and concealment, the enemy is used to mingle-up his identity with the environment and therefore one cannot identify one's enemy and his weapons and equipments which he has concealed with every precaution as visibility is poor.

2. **Restricted Largest Force and Vehicles:** On account of limited roads, footpaths, poor visibility and accessibility one cannot employ the numbers of vehicles and deploy the largest force, at a time in jungles, as in plain warfare. And even it is not feasible for safety and security; they may be a subject to be ambushed. The only remedy is to deploy the troops in a small group like sections, platoons and even same time company. In jungle warfare one have no alternative rather than deploy one's forces in scattered form and therefore it is being said that jungle warfare is a warfare of skirmishes.
3. **Safety and Security of Soldiers**: Maintain the safety and security of soldiers from wild animals. Creatures are one of the major problems. In jungle warfare as mentioned earlier it is very difficult to identify your enemy. Similarly, you cannot guess about "Ambush" being laid by enemy. Owing to accuracy in camouflage and concealment being managed by enemy, your soldiers may be the subject to be "ambushed" and it will be a great loss of manpower. So in jungle warfare the safety and security of soldiers poses such threat and the best option is to be "vigilant".
4. **Challenges to Engineers:** The engineering force has to do a lot of things. To clear the jungles and mines set by the enemy and similarly to spread up the mines at the possible routes of enemy. If the bridge is destroyed then they have to provide substitute arrangement to cross the rivers and streams. As the roads are very limited in jungles so the engineering force is supposed to prepare the temporary road, tracks for vehicles. [18] Without active role of Engineering force an advance in jungle would be difficult.
5. **Problem of Intercommunication**: As it is mentioned earlier, jungle warfare is a different kind of warfare. Like plain warfare we cannot employ the largest body of troops in jungle warfare, it has to be scattered in the environment of Nature and to be split up into small groups. In view of this fact, it becomes highly essential

to maintain the active communication within these small groups which is scattered in nature. To transmit the informations about further course of action and maintain the command, control and communication the effective signal network is required which would be able to provide these vital communication, facilities without disturbances neither by the enemy and nor by environment. But the jungle environment is not feasible for effective communication system which offers a number of challenges to the Signal department.

6. **Problem of Concentration of Fire Power:** In view of limited roads, routes and transportation, it is very difficult to employ the heavy fire weapons against enemy. The question how to organise the heavy fire against enemy remains unanswered. Tanks and even heavy artillery can be employed but it requires safety, security, secrecy, otherwise before its use it may be the subject of anti-tank guns, mines or air strike by the enemy. [19]

7. **Challenges to Air Power:** The air power has definitely a crucial role in this jungle warfare. The overall success of its role depends on intelligence i.e. exact and detailed information about the enemy in every respect. To provide close support to ground forces by carrying out tactical bombing against the enemy, the detail knowledge about location of the enemy is required. Taking off in the air, and then landing, dropping of the goods and commodities at Dropping zones (D.Z.) and to carry out casualties and wounded soldiers for further procedure are supposed to be looked after by airforce. [20] In jungle it is difficult for aircraft to perform all these responsibilities but this can be managed by Helicopter.

12.4.3 Logistic Problems

The Logistic problems in jungle warfare can be summarised as follows :

1. **Transportation:** In view of the limited roads and restrictions on employment of required vehicles it is difficult to carry out logistics supply.

Then only option remains before logistic management is mules, horse, local population, light vehicles etc.

2. **Medical Facilities:** As discussed earlier that a jungle is a home of diseases like, flew, cold, temperature, malaria and similarly bite by creatures especially snakes as well as dysentery, diarrhea. The medical services are supposed to have foresight and be prepared accordingly well in advance.
3. **Problem of Construction Material:** In order to strengthen the defensive position, the combat forces require variety of construction materials for observation post and bunkers. It should be prevented carefully that nobody will cut the trees for preparation of bunker or Observation Post (O.P.) because it will indicate your presence and enemy will come to know about your existence. So, therefore, the construction material should be made available in full stock.
4. **Need for Careful Planning:** In jungle warfare planning for logistics at every level has to be made with detail study. Every possibility has to be taken into consideration like accidents, various diseases, injuries, then stocking of food, ammunition, fodder for animals etc.[21] The logistic planning at every level should have substitute arrangement to cope-up with any peril.

12.5 High Altitude (Snow) Warfare

High Altitude (Snow) Warfare

1. Time Bound Accessibility	1. Problems of Observation	1. Limitations on transport
2. Limited Roads	2. Problems of Firepower	2. Water Supply
3. Transportation	3. Communication Problems	3. Stocking a Critical Problem.
4. Lack of Water	4. Defending Passes and Height	4. Warm kit / Clothing
5. Dumping Problem	5. Infantry, best remedy	5. Geo-medical Problems
6. Set of Problems for Field Commander	6. Limitation of vehicles 7. Air Support	6. Logistics role of Air Power

12.5.1 Characteristics

1. **Time Bound Accessibility**: The "High Altitude" area is absolutely unfavourable to the "development" and offers a number of challenges to the human beings. Accessibility is restricted by this difficult terrain. You can have access from September to November, whatever may be the aim —either conduct of war, dumping of goods and commodities or transportation.

   Throughout the year only three months i.e. September, October and November are ideal for war and human activities. And rest of the months you can find snowfall, rain and flood due to snow melting. It means you can have an access only three months tentatively throughout the year. This might be the reason that the Chinese had launched a massive attack in the Himalayan territory of India during 20th October to November in 1962.

2. **Limited Roads**: In this area roads are not adequate and construction of road is a very difficult task, it would be risky, costly and critical. And whatever roads are available you cannot use the heavy vehicles, only jeep and three-ton vehicles can be employed up to the height of seven to eight thousand feet only. Beyond seven-eight thousand feet your heavy vehicles may fall down in the valleys. Thus the roads are very limited in this area.

3. **Transportation:** Transportation upto the top of the mountains or our position at the height, is one of the difficult task. It can be carried out by light vehicles, mules and even local population. The local population is very much habitual and familiar with the mountains and have a potential to carry out goods and commodities upto the desired height. [22] Use of air power is limited and will depend upon the situation in every respect.

4. **Lack of Water:** Water which is available in mountainous areas may be due to rainfall or snow melting process. Such water is not purified and therefore not advisable for drinking purpose. If you intend to use it for drinking then the process of purification has to be done. Otherwise

the water has to be carried out from below the mountain to the required heights.

The water which has been brought from the bottom through pipeline upto certain heights can freeze during severe winter or cold and even due to sudden changes in weather conditions.

5. **Dumping Problem**: One of the major characteristics of this area is "snowfall" which creates the problem for dumping of food, ammunition and various goods and commodities. By excavation of the surface of mountain, if you intend to store the food, ammunition in excavated place, very soon it will be wet due to dampness of the ground by snow-melting and useless due to constant seeping of snow water. So owing to snowfall dumping of ammunition, food, goods and commodities becomes one of the genuine problems in mountains.
6. **Set of Problems for Field Commander**: The hills, chains of the mountain ranges with their slopes, lack of levelled space, sparse population, weather, vegetation, poor accessibility and communication, in a nutshell their characteristics of high altitude pose a number of problems for Field Commander. And all these regional characteristic-oriented problems can be sorted out by detailed study and preparation accordingly.

12.5.2 Tactical Problems

As regards the characteristics of this high altitude area, it offers a number of challenges to the field commander and his force. The "combat forces" in this high-altitude have to face the following difficulties i.e. tactical problems.

1. **Problem of Observation**: The mountain "relief" offers good opportunity for observation but in some cases it is restricted specially on reverse and convex slopes and valley bottoms due to interlocking spurs.
2. **Problem of Fire Power**: Basically this area offer uninterrupted fire, subject to the occupied position i.e. place-location of fire. Otherwise the field of fire is also

restricted in mountain terrain. It is difficult to carry out the heavy artillery or weapons upto the required heights and hence it has to be managed by light weight but effective fire-arms and weapons. High trajectory and crest clearance guns and heavy mortars are more effective than conventional artillery in this area.

3. **Communication Problems:** This high altitude area does affect on line of sight radio equipments and reduces short range transmission distances. This high altitude poses a number of technical problems in smooth functioning of communication system. Telephone, wireless, mobile get lot of disturbances due to the height of mountains and jungle i.e. trees in the altitude area.

   And there are chances that your communication lines may be disturbed by the enemy. In this high altitude area, it is very difficult to re-establish or maintain the intercommunication within the established various branches of the combat forces.

4. **Defending Passes and Heights:** The "Passes" in high altitude area hold their own geostrategic significance. From tactical point of view the passes are most important in this high altitude warfare. Synonymously some of the high hills also holds its importance during tactical movements of the combat forces. The "party" who has already occupied the "Heights" can enjoy the tactical consideration and dominate the enemy. If you intend to grab the "Height" from the enemy, dislocate him for his tactically sound position. Being an attacker you have to start from the bottom and thrash out the enemy from his tactically sound position. You will have to pay very heavy price in terms of casualties of the soldiers and ammuniation.[23] During Kargil war of India-Pakistan in 1999, the same experience had been experienced by Indian troops. So in high altitude warfare certain passes and heights have their own importance and the troops have to be defended successfully.

5. "**Infantry" Best Remedy:** Without "Infantry" soldiers, the war in high altitude area is highly impossible. To

climb up to such risky and critical heights, an intensive training is required. Physically rough, tough and acclimatised soldiers is the asset of the high altitude warfare. Whereas without such tough physical features the required training, conduct of war in mountains and as well as snow-covered terrain is difficult. [24]

6. **Limitation:** In high altitude warfare there are a number of restrictions and limitations. In view of the limited roads and series of the mountains you cannot employ more vehicles, troops at a time. This warfare is not mobile and speedy like plain warfare. And normally tanks cannot be employed at such great height but some exceptional cases are found in the history of warfare. Celebrated soldiers like General Thimayya had employed the tank upto (Josila pass) 1600 feet high during Indo-Pak war of 1947-48. [25] Besides, there is problem like absence of cover or concealment etc.
7. **Air Support:** Close support to ground forces even in high altitude area is one of the task of air power. But air power has a number of limitations and restrictions in this terrain as for example "fog" reduces the visibility. Wind will affect the speed of aircraft and assistance or support from the air power may be acquired but subject to "local geography". If the climatic condition is suitable, the "airpower" can play a determinant role in high altitude warfare. During Kargil war of 1999 Indian Air Force had given close support to the Infantry which produced the intended result.[26]

12.5.3. Logistic Problems

In high altitude warfare "Logistic Problem" is more severe and acute as compared to plain and desert warfares. Lack of effective assimilation process, poor development and low density of population in peripheral area can have negative implications on logistic management. It has a great question mark before the logistic management that how to procure all the required goods and commodities at such great heights? Operating logistic supply in this difficult terrain itself is a great challenge before mankind. Problems of logistic supply are as follows:

1. **Limitation of Transport**: How to carry out required goods for the combat forces upto certain height with safety, security and risk. After seven thousand feet the heavy vehicles cannot be employed, light vehicles, mules and even local resident of the area would solve the purpose. Over and above, the mules, local residents and light vehicles have certain limitations. For example, mule cannot carry more than 50 to 80 kg weight at a time. So limitation of every option has to be considered.
2. **Water Supply:** How to supply water upto the required or expected height is another major problem. From the ground, the water supply through pipes can be managed but upto certain height only, not upto the desired point. During cold or winter such pipelines can get frozen and ultimately blocked. Moreover, whatever water is available at such altitude is not feasible for drinking purpose.
3. **Stocking—A "Critical Problem":** On account of geographical circumstances, for near about 7/8 months throughout the year, the area is cut off from the rest of the country. It is very difficult to dump the essential goods and commodities at safe and secured place. In this area you cannot find such safe and secure place which could solve your purpose. And owing to constant seeping of snow-water you cannot dump it in a deep trench or bunkers. How and where stocking arrangement can be made? It's a critical problem before the logistic management.
4. **Warm Kit-Clothing:** This high altitude area receives heavy rainfall as well as snowfall during winter. Due to rainfall and snowfall this area becomes very cold and we require full set of (top to bottom) warm clothing including mattresses, pillows and blankets. Without warm clothing it would be very difficult to carry out a daily routine smoothly and effectively. In addition to this, fuel i.e. dry-wood, kerosene has to be managed before the monsoon and snowfall.

5. **Geo-Medical Problems:-** In accordance with regions, you can find a variety of health problems. On the mountains "lack of water" is a genuine problem; therefore, soldiers in this area have no water for taking bath. So due to circumstances they have to stay for a couple of days without a bath, and hence they are likely to suffer from skin diseases. Another problem for medical services is — chest, breathing, dehydration, severe temperature etc.[27] So medical services have to meet all these problems and be prepared accordingly well in advance.

6. **Logistics Role of Air Power**: Air force has a number of technical difficulties and due to variation in climate there are certain limitations. Despite this fact they have to perform their role of collection of casualties and seriously wounded soldiers for further procedure. Another acute problem is to find out a "Dropping zone" and drop the food packets and other required goods commodities, arms and ammunition etc. [28]

Footnotes

1. Lt. Col M. G. Abhyankar, Retd, *Defence Principles and Organisation,* Usha Prakashan, Pune University, Ganeshkhind, Pune-7, 1974, pp.141-42.
2. General Retd. K.V. Krishna Rao, *Prepare or Perish: A Study of National Security,* Lancer Publisher, New Delhi,1991, pp.133-34.
3. Lt. Col M. G. Abhyankar, Retd, *op. cit.,* p.143.
4. Lt.Gen. R. S. Singh, Retd., "Infantry: Queen of Battle", *U.S.I Journal*, April-June 1990, Kashmir House, Rajaji Marg, New Delhi, pp.172-73.
5. "Interview/Discussion" with Dr.J.A. Khan, Reader, on 28/7/06, Deptt. Of Defence and Strategic Studies, Bhonsala Military College Nasik-5. (M.S.) author of *Air Power and Challenges to IAF*, Published by A.P.H., New Delhi 2004.
6. A.L. Venkateshwaran, *India's Defence Organisation,* Hindi Grantha Academy, Bhopal, 1973, pp.15-16.

7. Lt. Col. M. G. Abhyankar, Retd., *op. cit.*, p.144.
8. J.A. Khan, *op. cit.*, dated 28th July 2006.
9. Lt.Col. M.G. Abhyankar, Retd., *op.cit.*, p.145-146.
10. Lt. Gen R. S. Singh, Retd., *op. cit.*, p.173.
11. Surendranath Sen, *Introduction: To The Art of Warfare*, Sterling Publisher, New Delhi, 1979, p.198.
12. S. T. Das, *Tactical Military Operation*, Sagar Publication, New Delhi, 1972. pp.5-6
13. Lt.Col. M. G. Abhyankar, Retd., *op. cit.*, p.145-146
14. Louis C. Peltier and G. Etzel Pearcy, *Military Geography*, East-West Press, Montieth Road, Chennai 8, 1981, p.59.
15. Lt. Col. M. G. Abhyankar, Retd., *op.cit.*, p.147-148.
16. Captain Raja Limaye, "Environment as a Factor of Warfare," *SAKAL*, Pune, Sunday, dated 26th April 1998.
17. A.P. Choudhary, *Military Geography*, Nirali Prakashan, 1995, Pune, India, pp.41-43.
18. S.T. Das, *op.cit*, 1972, pp..5-6.
19. Lt.Col. M.G. Abhyankar, Retd., *op.cit.*, p.156.
20. J.A. Khan, *op. cit*, Discussion/Interview, dated 28/7/2006.
21. Lt. Col. M. G. Abhyankar, Retd., *op. cit*, p.157-158
22. Prof. S. R. Latkar and A.S. Apate, *Political Geography*, Vidya Prakashan, Nagpur, 1998, pp. 57-58.
23. S.T. Das, *op.cit.*, 1972, pp.7-8.
24. Lt.Gen. R.S. Singh, Retd., pp.142-143.
25. Lt.Col. M.G. Abhyankar, Retd., *op. cit.*, p.79-80.
26. J.A. Khan, *op.cit.*, Discussion/Interview, dated 28/7/2006.
27. Lt.Col. M.G. Abhyankar, *op. cit.*, p.152-53.
28. J.A. Khan, *op. cit.*, Discussion/Interview, dated 28/7/2006.

✤ ✤ ✤

13

MAN AND ENVIRONMENT

13.1 INTRODUCTION

Man and environment are two most important factors. It is vital to study the "relationship" between both of them. The study of social sciences—earth sciences—would not be complete without due consideration of man and environment. The history of human being shows that man was a part of "Nature" but today the picture is critically bleak. On account of "modernisation", man has become seperate from nature. Though man has mobility and he can migrate from one place to another; but wherever he goes he has to adjust himself to the new environment.

It is the "requirements" of human being due to which the fundamental changes have occurred in relationship between man and environment. It is apparent that due to urbanisation, industrialisation and day-by-day increasing population, the ecological balance has been disturbed severely. But the fact cannot be denied that progress and human life are affected directly, vigorously and persistently by environmental factors. No major activity of human society is independent of physical environment.

13.2 Determinism v/s Possibilism

It is very difficult to justify which one is first—"egg or chicken"? Synonymously it's difficult to judge whether

Nature (Determinism) is superior or Man (Possibilism) is superior. It is a study of interaction between Man and Nature.

This is to be considered that physical factors of Environment govern human attitude, habits and even nature. In other words history, culture, living style and stages of development of a state, nation or social group are exclusively governed by physical factors of the environment. The well-known Geopolitician **Ratzel** supports this fact. According to him:

"The mode of life of the people and the stage of development are closely influenced by the physical features."

Prof. Mackinder, Chisholm Davies, Bowman also had agreed that the progress of society would be achieved with deterministic approach. It is the climate which has the influence on physical properties of soil which ultimately determines the cropping pattern, dietary habits, overall physique and attitude. For example, people of hill tracts normally have relative isolation which leads one to be orthodox and conservative. People from hill tracts have a suspicious attitude towards the stranger. These people are more sensitive in traditions and do not tolerate any sort of criticism by anybody else.

The people of the plain, like Europeans are energetic, serious, thoughtful rather than emotional. They are bold and adventurous. The people of Europe went out for exploration and discoveries of new territories, land, Islands in Asia and Africa. So the result of traveling, survey for exploration and discovery culminated into the rise of possibilism. In the process of exploration and discoveries, geography has played determinant role—it is the geography which had a role of investigator in order to understand the nature of transition from "Natural" to the cultural landscape. [1]

Lucian Febvre is one of the followers of "Possibilism" who believes that Man is superior to "Nature". Lucian, explained various stages of development of various civilization and societies. This approach of interpretation of history is considered as "Possibilism". **According to Lucian** "Nature does not drive men along a particular road but it offers a number of opportunities, Man is free to choose out of it". **According to the followers of posssibilism,** "Nature is never more than an advisor". It has been said that necessity is the mother of invention but as per followers of possibilities "there are no necessities but everywhere there are possibilities. The range of possibilities is everywhere but it is relevant to subject to input cost and will-power.

For example, Israel by virtue of sophisticated Agro-Technology cultivated the various crops in barren land. Can we afford such heavy input cost? It depends on the will-power and capacity to bear input cost.

Vidal de Lablache one of the scholars explains that possibilism means to minimise the influence of environment on human activities. Some of the people or even group may be influenced deeply but some of them can prove better than others which depends upon a "ratio of influence". We can find the variation between various groups or tribes in the same environment especially in attitude, habits, values etc. For example, in Maharashtra before the birth of Shivaji as compared to Mawale people, Bhonsale, Jadhav, Shinde, Ghorphade, Nimbalkar were well reputed as warriors. The followers of possibilism are firm with their opinion, according to them man is the builder and earth changer and the relationship between man and environment is not static. The natural environment has been modified and even verified by technological invention and improvement. The construction of Suez canal is one of the "wonders" and distinct example for the above mentioned fact.

Man, material or physical progress is largely determined by his success in adjusting his action with available physical environment. The followers of possibilism confess that the opportunities offered by any environment are not equal. Over and above it is to be considered that whatever the progress may be attained by human being he will not be having upper hand over "Nature". Science and Technology has only minimised the influence of environment on "Man".[2]

13.3 War and Environment

13.3.1 Significance

War and environment has a close relationship like man and environment. The environment has occupied a significant place in the process of "Tactical Planning". While planning for conduct of war it is vital to take into account environmental factors such as Rivers, Seacoast, Mountains, Streams, Altitude, Air-Climate. It is the strategists and tacticians who suppose to have an idea about the use of environmental factors during actual conduct of war. The field Commander or local leader should have vast knowledge of local environment, he should be able to use maximum environmental factors for the conduct of war.

The history of war and environment begins from the ancient period. The brilliant war philosopher Kautilya who explained in detail about it, in his self-written literature "Kautilya's Arthasastra". According to environment he had categorised the types of forts i.e. Jal Durga, Parvat Durga, Dhaman Durga (fort in desert).

1. Rivers: In the past, during war environmental factors had proved a genuine cause for "Havoc". During the battle of Hydaspus (Jhelum) in 326 B.C., Alexander while crossing the Jhelum River had lost the soldiers alongwith weapons and equipments. In the same capacity during the third battle of Panipat in A.D. 1761 Ahmed Shah Abdali also lost the men and material while crossing the Yamuna River.

2. Climate: Though man has used environmental factors to attain victory but due to lack of knowledge, or consideration and even poor planning, climate would prove as a determinant factor. In this context a "Russian Campaign" by Napoleon Bonaparte is to be considered a distinct one. Due to the vast size of Russia and severe winter he was unable to proceed and at last dropped his idea to conquer Russia. During World War II, Hitler also bound up the operation, Barbarossa, which was started against U.S.S.R.

3. Dense Forest, Deep Valleys and Mountains: During the battle of Pratapgadh, King Shivaji being a tactician forced Afzal Khan indirectly to begin war in the territory of Jawali. Shivaji, great leader of Maratha kingdom, had successfully used environmental factors to trap the enemy. It was possible for him to defeat Afzal Khan due to co-ordination and combination between existing resources and available environment. Shivaji had utilised every possible environmental factor during the battle of Pratapgadh; therefore, he won against Afzal Khan.

During America's "Vietnam war" in the eighties, the local people (Guerrilla) by taking advantages of the dense forest, valley and altitude, defeated the U.S. Army. By virtue of environmental factors, Vietnam forced the American Army to accept the defeat.

4. Moonlight, Wind and Low tide of the Sea: Moonlight, direction of the wind and low tide can play a crucial role during war. History of warfare has recorded this fact. Moonlight can offer a "visibility" to crew, pilot, driver and even soldiers to carry out their task as per direction and speed of wind. It can affect the mobility and even clear the smoke screen during "assault". And in the same capacity high and low tide of the sea also has some tactical advantage and disadvantages.

During World War II the Allied Forces had plan to cross the English Channel and land at Normandy coast and obviously German had erected strong defence arrangement to counter Allied Forces. German had deployed Artillery directed towards sea and throughout the seacoast and spread up the mines. To counter the German preparation the environmental factors were intensively used by the Allies. After detailed study and analysis of "Nature-Environmental" factors, the D-Day was finalised and that was 6th of June 1944. By the midnight of 5th June and early dawn of 6th June 1944, the Parachute of Allies landed at the rear front of the Germans and attacked. Similarly, the other Parachute landed at Normandy. By virtue of low tide the mines spread by the Germans were "neutralised" by the Allied Forces. The "speed of wind" helped to clear the smoke screen which was already created by the use of "Bombing and Artillery". And moonlight offered the visibility. So this spectacular victory was achieved by Allied Forces owing to successfull use of environmental factors.[3]

5. Creatures and Collection of water: Man has successfully used the environmental factors including flora, fauna, water creatures for conduct of war. Mules, camels, horses, elephants are used according to suitability e.g. mules are used in high altitude area for transportation. Camel is used as a vehicle for transportation in desert or dunes. Camel is called a ship of desert. Pigeon were intensively employed by the kings during ancient period for "communication" purpose during peace and war. Various poisonous creatures—animals are employed for biological warfare even today. "Water" is an essential factor for every human being. As per changes of variable situation on battlefield somebody had the benefit and someone had defeated or defended on account of water. During Indo-Pak war of 1965 Indian Army was unable to cross the Ichogil canal to capture the Lahore city of Pakistan. Camel, Dams, Rivers, Channels have been great and effective hazards in the process of conduct of war. During Gulf war of 1990 America and her Allied forces destroyed near about forty bridges of Iraq which were constructed over Ufratis River. By "collection of water" during Indo-Pak war of 1965 at Khemkaran sector, Pattan tanks of Pakistani forces were captured by Indian Army and this was possible due to only tactical use of water against enemy.

13.4 War and its Impact on Environment

[Historical Evaluation]. As we consider "war" as an ancient phenomenon, the references are made available. During Ramayana period when Hanuman went to Sri Lanka as an envoy of Rama, it was Hanuman who set Lanka on fire. So this act of Hanuman had a negative repercussion on the environment of Sri Lanka. There were numbers of incidents regarding negative implications of war on environment during medieval period of history.

First and Second World Wars have the witnesses for negative implications of war on environment. During World War I, "Trench Warfare" had one of the great causes for "Ecological Imbalance". To prepare the trenches and survive in it, the environment was disturbed. In order to restore the "Mobility" on this western front during World War I the Germans had used various gases against the Allied forces which had a severe impact on soldiers and environment. During World War II British Royal Air Force and the American Air Force as a part of joint venture, had carried out "Strategic Bombing" in deep territory of Germany. This strategic bombing did great havoc to the manpower and environment of Germany.

The World War II had come to an end by the origin of new trend of warfare and i.e. "Nuclear Warfare". The invention of Nuclear warfare has a great setback for human being. It has a lot of progressive uses for human being. The first use of nuclear weapons at Nagasaki and Hiroshima is an evidence how far these nuclear weapons are "harmful" to Humanity and Environment. Owing to "shock, heat and radiation" of the nuclear bomb, dropped by America, thousands of peoples lost their lives and surrounding land became infertile. And even today not a single blade of grass grows over there. People are suffering from liver diseases and cancer even today; the Americans have introduced new bomb and i.e. "Neutron Bomb" which has a basic aim to destroy the human being and environment.[4]

It was U.S.A. again who had done a great havoc to man and environment of Vietnam during war in the seventies against Guerrillas of Vietnam. Americans used the variety of destructive bombs in a large quantity due to it—forests, flora, fauna, birds, wild animals and vegetation were destroyed.

"Iraq" also had a negative role for destruction and devastation of environment and imbalancing an ecological balance during 1992. To counter the U.S., Iraqi forces set on fire the maximum oil wells of Kuwait during their withdrawal which had culminated in merging of sulphur and carbon dioxide, dust with environment. On 27th January 1992 more than hundred crores barrels of oil intentionally spilled the sea due to which the Persian Gulf and Arab countries were seriously affected. Owing to this "oil" in sea water, marine life creatures, maritime resources and surrounding environment was badly affected. The people and environment of this region had faced severe consequences of gulf war of 1992.

Sum-up: By the following activities/movements of war:

a) Land Mines against Man and Vehicles
b) Use of Artillery
c) Bombardment
d) Use of Ammunition
e) Use of Chemical and Biological Weapons

An environment has the following negative implications by above mentioned movements of war:

1. Land becomes a subject of digging and excavation.
2. Infertility of soil.
3. Destruction and devastation of Jungle—forest, flora, fauna and various creatures.
4. Disturbances of Natural cycle of Monsoon or rainfall.
5. Environment pollution and ecological imbalance.
6. Loss, diseases and negative impact on human being and various organism.

13.5 Environment: As a Factor of National Security

13.5.1 Importance

Security—the term has a wider meaning with multi-dimensional scope. Everybody is bothered about "security" i.e. Industrial, Socio-cultural, Economical, Political, National. The politicians are always anxious about "security of Vote

Bank". The government is aware of the "National Security" and dealing consecutively with insurgency, terrorism, communal riots...exclusively. But like India, no one visualised the seriousness of "Environment Pollution". The safe, secure and non-polluted environment is most important, without it healthy survival of human being is not possible. The security of environment is as important as that of "human being". So environment should be pollution free, safe and secure and hence it has to be considered as a factor of National security.

"Pollution" of air, water-river is not a new phenomenon; even deforestation is not a new one. The Industrial Revolution, inventions, process of Industrialisation in Europe during Medieval period have to be considered as the beginning of "Pollution". The 20th century was a milestone in this regard, during America's Vietnam war in the seventies the "Jungles" of Vietnam were subject to destruction and devastation. The seriousness of this Environment factor was assumed during Gulf war of 1991-92 when Iraq had lit on the maximum oil wells on fire and Kuwait had spilled the oil in the sea. Owing to this Iraqi's act, an environment had the long term and serious consequences. [6] Since this episode safe, secure and non-polluted environment has emerged as a factor of National security.

By virtue of the recent awareness about environment it is apparent that paradigm shift took place from State (institution) security to security of environment and of human being (individual). The security and safety of environment has come-up as an anchor in security management of the country. With safe and secure environment if human being cannot survive, then how the security of a state would be established. After all national security or survival as a "nation" depends on healthy citizens and soldiers. Therefore "Environmental Security" has forcefully come-up as one of the core issues of national security. The environment in which we live should be free from pollution and is comfortable for every citizen—human being.

13.5.2 Pollution: Nature, Causes and Problems

Once upon a time man was a part of nature and very friendly with her. But it is observed that "industrialisation, urbanisation and deforestation" have changed the relationship between man and environment. Now man is working as an enemy of environment; this anti-act of human being raised the question of survival of himself.

Logically "Environment and Development" have no contradiction, if you have proper planning and foresight, then it won't be and need not clash with each other. The causes of environment pollution need to be analysed on the basis of material facts. The overall causes of environment pollution lies in "large increasing population" which requires "more" food, raw material, resources, water, shelter, job, fuel. These endless and day-by-day increasing demands of man have posed a "serious challenge" to natural reproduction capacity of the earth. The "over" and misuse of environmental factors have savagely damaged the ecological balance. It is vital to maintain the balance between available resource on this earth and existing population. After all it should be remembered that "Nature" has her own methods of controlling, balancing and checking.[7]

Anyhow, fact cannot be denied that rapid industrialisation, urbanisation, deforestation, and the increasing population have created a major environmental crisis in the world. Pollution is there in the atmosphere (air), on land, in the seas and rivers. Our pure and fresh air is being polluted by smoke, gases and chemicals puffed out by vehicles and industries. In addition to this you can be disturbed by noise pollution i.e. noise of various vehicles, machines, loudspeakers and even crackers. Despite the scarcity of water as a worldwide problem, we cannot find easily clean water point. Tonnage of wastage material from industries, which has very poisonous and harmful chemicals are casually dumped into lakes, streams, rivers, and seas. This water pollution kills the water-creatures, flora, fauna and other marine lives.

Over and above, we must remember the severe implications of such pollution on human body. Polluted air becomes poisonous and harmful; owing to polluted air—millions of premature deaths are recorded. It is needless to mention that automobile exhaust is one of the major causes of various allergies and respiratory illness. In the environment the ratio of CO2 is being increased which has negative effects on "Green House" and "Temperature" is increasing year after year. Owing to this ozone layer over the Antarctica region little bit destroyed i.e. the creation of ozone hole. This ozone hole is the effect of Chloro-carbon and Chloro-Fluoro methane gases in the atmosphere.

Ozone layer of the earth is protecting us from the radiation of the sun. If the ozone layer is destroyed fully, the human being will have to pay very heavy price i.e. human race will 'perish'. Because of increasing temperature the snow tremendously melted from 1980 to 2005, 20 lakh sq kms ice has been melted. If this continues then in the 21st century all snow will be vanished. We must consider alarming situation and act accordingly. Due to this increasing temperature there will be serious threat to Islands and costal territories. In future it will be submerged under the sea. Even the glacier in Himalayan region is also melting rapidly which will hamper water supply for the concerned rivers.[8]

Taking into consideration of various kinds of pollution and its severe impact on human body and environment, we must acknowledge the environment as a factor of National security and act positively. If the environment remains non-polluted, safe and secure, then only we would be able to maintain the healthy and physically stout soldiers for the armed forces to preserve national security. It can be rightly said in this context that "Health is Wealth".

In future unhealthy and tired environment and lack of fresh air, which is one of the numerous causes for diseases, may give rise to strategic problems like eco-refugees, food deficiency and it may mount up the tensions within Nations-States. The environmental degradation is conducive to conflict. Environmental security is covered with environmental causes of conflict i.e. health, life and economy of the people as well as State. Devastation of an environment may cause the immigration of the people from one country to another to avail safe and secure environment and it may create strategic complications within the concerned states. Therefore, the environmental degradation as a security concern is fully consistent with National Security.

Footnotes

1. Majid Hussain, *Human Geography*, Rawat Publication, New Delhi, 1994, pp.18-21.
2. *Ibid.*, pp.29-33.
3. V.Y. Jadhav, "War & Enviornment", *Maharashtra Geography: Science Journal*, Vol.XIII, No.2, July-Dec 1999, Marathi Version, pp.121-23.
4. Captain Raja Limaye, "Environment As a Factor of War", *Sakal*, Nashik Edition, 26th April 1998.
5. Mishra Surendrakumar, *Gulf War and Its Impact*, Radha Publication, New Delhi, 1993,. p.190-91.
6. Varsha Gajendra Gadkar, "Assurance for Security," *Sakal*, Nashik Edition, dated 21/4/1998.
7. Sunita Narayan, "First Pollution and Then Solution: Is It Affordable?" *Sakal, Weekly Journal* , Mumbai, 14th June 2006, pp.6-10.
8. Mohan Apte, "National Disaster Year," *Lokrang*, Sunday, dated 25th Dec 2005, Nashik.

✣ ✣ ✣

14

DISASTER AND CIVIL DEFENCE

14.1 INTRODUCTION

"Civil Defence" coordinates the relationship between civilian and military, specially during war period. The term "civil defence" itself indicates the meaning i.e. defence of the citizen, by the citizen, for the citizen. In a wider context "civil defence" means the measures adopted by the civilian population of respective Government, local self government bodies and the voluntary organisations etc. [1] The ultimate aim of civil defence is to minimise the effects of enemies' action on men and material during war and restore the normalcy in essential services.

14.1.2 Historical Account

During World War II when the British Royal Air Force and United States Air Force carried out "Strategic Bombing" against Germany, at that time Germans had a civil defence organisation. Though it failed to serve the purpose, it must be considered that this was the first attempt. Even Japanese civil defence organisation was not that much adequate. [2] In India there is no practical experience except air raids on Calcutta and the east sea coast. On 24th October 1941 the civil defence department was constituted. During Chinese invasion certain measures of civil defence were adopted.

During Indo-Pak wars of 1965 and 1971 the civil defence organisation had a role which was played effectively.

14.2 Significance of the Civilian Population

In modern warfare "Civilian Population" has a determinant role without which conduct of war is highly impossible. It is being considered that behind one combat soldier ten persons are working in various industries, mines, fields and depots, administrative installations etc. The population is a core part and vital in overall process of the conduct of modern warfare. The morale, discipline, safety and adequate training with security of the population must be taken into consideration, only then the Government will be able to cope-up with the situation whatever may be the case. [3]

14.3 Structure of Civil Defence Organisation

India's Case: At the centre "Civil Defence" falls under the purview of Ministry of Home Affairs, Government of India. It has civil defence committee which is chaired by Home Secretary. And the representatives from the various ministries are supposed to be the members of this civil defence committee. This committee gives an advice to the Government of India on the issues and policy matters of civil defence. The Ministry of Home Affairs also has another "Civil Defence Joint Planning Staff" — the Director General of civil defence is the chairman and representative at deputy secretary level from each central government ministries. [4] This committee deals with coordination of all civil defence measures. The following chart shows the nature of civil defence organisation in India.

Ministry of Home Affairs

(Government of India)

- Chairman (Home Secretary) Civil Defence Committee
  - Members:- Representatives from various Ministries of the Central Government.
- Chairman Director General of Civil Defence
  - Civil Defence Joint Planning Staff Committee.
    - One representative at Deputy Secretary level from each Ministry of Central Government.

Government of India

Ministry of Home Affairs

- Director General of Civil Defence
  - Directors (State Level)
    - District Magistrate (District Level)
      - Revenue Treasury (Dy Commissioner or Collector)
      - Police (D.S.P)
      - Medical Health (DMO or Civil Surgeon)
      - PWD (Executive Engineer)
      - Transport (RTO)
      - Education (DEO) or District Inspector of School
- National Civil Defence College and National Fire Service College, Nagpur.

In the light of the above chart it is clear that at the local level various existing Government Departments are responsible for organising suitable Civil Defence services. For example, the civil surgeon is to be appointed as an in-charge of casualty service. The regional transport officer i.e. R.T.O. is supposed to be the incharge of "Depot and Transport service" and so on. The District Magistrate is the controller of civil defence who is responsible for execution of civil defence measures vigorously. The S.P., P.W.D. Engineers, publicity officers are appointed by district magistrate as incharges of various civil defence services. [5] The civil defence services are as follows:

- Headquarters Service
- Warden Services
- Fire Fighting Services
- Casualties Services
- Communication Services
- Training Services
- Welfare Services
- Depot and Transport Services
- Salvage Services
- Corpse Disposal Services
- Supply Services
- Emergency Services during war
  (Rather than above services)

The civil defence organisation has to train the citizens even to deal with insurgents, terrorists, social evils, natural calamities etc. in a perfect manner. The citizens have to be literate in every respect and should be able to cope-up with any situation. They must be able to deal with situation: Pre-Attack/Natural Calamity, During attack or Calamity, Post attack/Calamity etc.

In India National Disaster Management may take over civil defence in near future.

Civil Defence Organisation has to deal with "disaster". The following chart shows the expected role by the civil defence organ.

14.4 Types of Disaster

DISASTER

Natural Calamities

a) Earthquake
Tsunami waves
Flood (Cyclone)
b) Heavy Rainfall
& Snowfall
c) landslide
Volcano etc.

War

a) Regular, declared war
Strategic Bombing
Air raid, mine-blast. etc.
b) Irregular, undeclared,
Insurgency, Terrorism
Anti-national or
Social elements
c) Nuclear War

14.4.1 Natural Calamities

Natural calamities forcefully came up as a great peril before the human being. Due to increasing and in some cases large population, the pressure upon existing resources is created. So constantly increasing demands of "natural Resources" have forced people to misuse the "Environment". Such a misuse of environment and resources severely disturbed the ecological balance which culminated in Natural calamities. Owing to ecological imbalance it is apparent that the incidents of natural calamity have increased tremendously since the last decade of the 20th century. Natural calamities cause great havoc to human beings, organisms and the wealth. It damages the organism, resources and wealth in every respect severely. According to Emergency Event Database Centre for Research on Epidemiology of Disaster (EM-DAT, CRED) University at Lauvain, Belgium and World Disaster Reports indicates the ratio and data of death affected by natural calamities. [6]

Natural disaster is a sort of destruction and devastation which cannot be controlled by human beings. Man cannot have upper-hand over nature. After Tsunami episode the Governments of respective countries have installed the infrastructure which would be able to inform in advance the alarming situation i.e. incoming Tsunami, cyclone etc. In future it will be proved that such infrastructure is practically capable to provide prior information about cyclone Tsunami etc. Whatever may be the fact but it can-not be denied that thousands of people have lost their lives during the recent Tsunami (cyclone). According to "Lokrang" dated 25th December 2005, Newspaper (Mumbai), the data of victims by Tusnami is as follows: (Data till 10th Feb 2005) [7]

Sr. No	Name of the country	Figures of deaths
1.	Indonesia	242347
2.	Sri Lanka	30957
3.	India	16389
4.	Thailand	5393
5.	Somalia	298
6.	Myanmar	61
7.	Maldives	82
8.	Malaysia	68
9.	Tanzania	10
10.	Bangladesh	2
11.	Kenya	1

Whatever may be the type of natural calamity, the fact remains crystal clear that it's a responsibility of the Government to cope-up with the situation, and to provide relief and restore the normalcy at the earliest possible. But how long and upto what extent the Government will succeed to perform the expected role in such critical conditions?After all Government does not hold a magic-stick. It must be accepted that peoples working in Governmental infrastructure / Organisation are also human. And as human beings they also have certain problems and limitations. They have to think and deal with calamities in a wider context and may not able to reach at a every affected point and hence every time Government should not be the subject of criticism. Now the pragmatic solution and active role of local residents of the concerned areas is expected. The local citizens and Non-Governmental Organisations must come forward and take the initiative during critical circumstances. During accident or natural calamities the civil defence services can be rendered.

14.4.2 War

War is one of the "instruments of policy", "means" and source of disaster through which a great havoc can be caused to the enemy's side. Civil defence organisation in India has an experience of 1962, 1965 and 1971 wars. But, now circumstances as well as nature of war also have changed. In view of the changing nature of war the civil defence organisation has to proliferate upto the grass roots of the society. Every citizen or local resident should become an active member of civil defence organisation. NGOs also have a wider scope to perform their expected role and responsibility during war and even at the time of natural calamities.

14.4.3 Challenge by Anti-National Elements

The rise of anti-national elements' separatist movements has posed a serious challenge to the society. Especially in India the North East region, Kashmir, Andhra Pradesh, Maharashtra, Madhya Pradesh states are being affected by anti-national elements i.e. insurgents, terrorist, militants, Naxalites. The Government will deal with them according to design and its own agenda but it's the local people who are becoming victims of terrorism, insurgency or Naxalite attack. Now it is an appropriate time that every citizen, local resident must come forward and become an active member of civil defence organisation. The people have to manage their defence by own efforts till the forces of Government arrived. In the eighties of the last century, terrorism was proliferated in Punjab vigorously. The people of Punjab got rid of terrorism only when they took initiative and came forward and fought against "terrorism". It is vital that every citizen, local resident should become an active member of civil defence organisation. The civil defence organisation should become a "Mass Movement" by the citizens against not only anti-national elements but social evils also.[8] In Kashmir an experiment has been conducted to manage the defence of the local residents by themselves only against terrorism. But it will take some time to get the positive result like Punjab episode. However, the geographical analysis of "conflict" of interest must be considered while dealing with anti-national elements.

14.4.4 Nuclear Warfare

The nuclear warfare is a subject of concern, perhaps, till, until, unless, as no incident of nuclear war occurred since Nagasaki and Hiroshima episode. It is very difficult to predict about "Nuclear War" with accuracy. After August 1945 there is no example of use of nuclear weapons. Whatever nuclear bombs were dropped over Nagasaki and Hiroshima, the more destructive bombs are being produced by nuclear powers, taking into consideration of Japanese devastation and destruction by nuclear bomb no one is willing to use nuclear weapons against their adversary. But we don't deny the possibilities of use of nuclear weapons due to revengeful attitude of the enemy in future.

The strategic problem of defence, offence, tactical problems of defence and offence in nuclear warfare poses a number of challenges before the Military Generals and the government. Apart from these problems of offence-defence during nuclear warfare, the question of civil defence remains unanswered that how to protect the civilian population from nuclear attack i.e. nuclear radiation, waves, blast, extreme heat etc. The nation has to develop the capacity to absorb the first nuclear strike of enemy by Anti Ballistic Missile system, radar, intelligence and so on. If the nation could absorb the first nuclear strike then only it can sustain. The second strike capability would depend on safety, security of target population and secrecy of nuclear arsenal.

The nuclear war will be different from conventional war, the time duration would be short but destruction will be more; large cities, population, radar, nuclear arsenal administrative installation will be the major targets. The repercussion will be horrible. The civil defence will have to face number of challenges specially.

Disposal of dead bodies

Procurement of a shelter (safe environment)

Removing debris

Availability of food and water

Medical relief

To face a nuclear attack and a cope-up with the post strike is inevitable; therefore, certain measures have to be taken by the Government along with Civil Defence Organisation. Possible measures to deal with post strike are as follows:

1. No nation can survive unless and until it possesses a second strike capability. The citizens should be literate about this kind of warfare. Lack of knowledge about the subject would cause a sort of apathy which may culminate in holocaust. To prevent such disaster by "Nuclear Attack", the common masses should be taken into confidence and educated adequately.
2. The maximum local residents should be well-trained to handle and operate various machine equipments, vehicle, without any difficulty. It will save time and produce positive result during emergency. Even this would be helpful to communicate with the people within the stipulated time.
3. Adequate water, food and first-aid kit should be preserved with safety, security and foresight. The controllers or authorities of civil defence must be able to deal with the post nuclear attack i.e. clearance of debris, casualties, procurement of food, water, shelter, medicines, various goods, commodities and essential equipments.

4. In nuclear warfare the most important aspect is "shelter". The shelter should be capable to protect the people from various reactions of nuclear bomb. Citizens should be trained accordingly, to seek the shelter. The possible shelter—deep trenches, bunkers, underground-railway or car parking, basement and in rural areas even silos may prove one of the best shelter place.[9] In future a provision of compulsory "nuclear shelter" must be introduced by the authorities of town planning in every city.

Footnotes

1. Lt. Col. M. G. Abhayankar, Retd., *Defence Principles and Organization*, Usha Prakashan, University of Pune, 1974, Pune 7, p.194.
2. Varma M.R.P. (Major), "Civil Defence in India: The Nature of the Problem", *USI Journal*, July-Sept 1994, Kashmir House, Rajaji Marg, New Delhi, pp-231-32.
3. *Ibid.*, p.234
4. *Cadet Hand Book*, N.C.C. Naval Wing, Mah. N.C.C. Naval Wing Bn., Mumbai, pp.315-16.
5. *Ibid.*, p.318.
6. Emergency Event Database Centre for Research on Epidemiology of Disaster [EM-DAT,CRED], University at Lauvain, Belgium and *World Disaster Report*, 2001, pp.27-28.
7. Mohan Apte, "Year of Natural Disaster" *Lokrang*, Newspaper, Mumbai, 25th Dec 2005.
8. Kiran Bedi's speech on 31/4/2006, 48th Anniversary, National Civil Defence College, Nagpur, (M.S.). Also *Lokmat*, Nashik Edition, Newspaper, dated 1/5/06.
9. Maj.Gen. Raman, "Civil Defence for a Nuclear Age: Indian Context," *USI Journal*, April-June1992, Kashmir House, Rajaji Marg, New Delhi-11, 1992, pp.153-456.

✣ ✣ ✣

BIBLIOGRAPHY

Primary Sources

1. Government of India, *The Sino-Indian Border Dispute: Question and Answer*, Ministry of Information and Broadcasting, Publication Division, 1962, New Delhi, India.
2. Government of India, *The Sino-Indian Boundary Text of Treaties: Agreement & Certain Exchange of Notes Relating to the Sino-Indian Boundary*, the Indian Society of International Law, Parliament Street, New Delhi, 1962, India.
3. Government of India, *White Paper–II*, Ministry of External Affairs, New Delhi, 1959, India.
4. 1st Maharashtra Naval Unit NCC, *Cadets Handbook*, Mumbai, NCC Office, Near Old Secretariat, Mumbai.
5. P C Dutta, *Arunachal Pradesh : An Overview*, Directorate of Research, Government of Arunachal Pradesh, Itanagar, 1993.

Secondary Sources

1. Adhikari, Shekhar, *Modern Strategic Thought: Machiavelli to Nuclear Warfare*, Kilosa Books, New Delhi 2004.
2. Adhikari Sudeepta, *Political Geography*, Rawat Publication, Jaipur, 2002.

3. Ahmed, Rashid, *Taliban: The Story of Afghan Warlords*, London, Pan Books, Pan, McMilan Ltd., 2001.
4. Athale, Anil Maj., *Arab-Israeli Wars 1967 and 1973*, I.S. Press, Calcutta, India,1980.
5. Abhyankar, M.G., Lt. Col. Retd., *Defence Principles and Organization*, Usha Prakashan, Ganeshkhind, Pune 7,1974.
6. Bhat, Sudhakar, *India and China*, Popular Book Service, New Delhi, 1967.
7. Bose, C.S., *Geography of the Himalaya*, National Book Trust, India, 1972.
8. Bruce W. Watson, *Military Lessons of the Gulf War*, Lancer International, New Delhi, 1991.
9. Cattrey, Matt and Chadwik, Frank, *Gulf War Fact Book*, Jupiter Publication, New Delhi,1991.
10. Chakrawati, P.C., *India-China Relations*, Mukhoopadhy Publisher, Calcutta, 1961.
11. Chaudhary, A.P., *Military Geography*, Nirali Prakashan, Pune, 1995, Marathi Edition.
12. Chaturvedi, Sanjay, *Drawing of Antarctica—A Geopolitical Analysis*, Segment Book Publishing, New Delhi, 1990.
13. Chitnis, S.G. Gp.Capt. Retd., and Chaudhary, A.P., *Indian Military History*, Archana Publication, Jalgaon, 1985.
14. Diwedi, R.L., *Fundamentals of Political Geography*, Chaitanya Publishing House, Allahabad 2, 1990.
15. Dixit. R.D., *Political Geography: The Discipline and Its Dimensions*, Tata McGrow Hill Publishers Company Ltd., New Delhi, 1972.
16. Das, S.T., *Tactical Military Operation*, Sagar Publication, New Delhi, 1912.
17. Das, S. T., *Geostrategy*, Kitab Mahal Agencies, Allahabad, 1986.

18. Earle Edward, *Makers of Modern Strategy*, Natraj Publication, Dehradun, 2003.

19. "Emergency Event Database" *Centre for Research on Epidemiology of Disaster*, EM- DAT- CRED, University of Lauvain, Belgium.

20. Ghai, U.R., *Inernational Politics*, New Academic Publishing Co., Jalandhar, 1989.

21. Gupta, Bharat Bhushan, *Arab-Israeli Relations*, Ashish Pub. House, New Delhi, 1978.

22. Heller, Mark A., *A Palestine State: The Implications for Israel*, University Press, Britain, 1983.

23. Hussain, Majid, *Human Geography*, Rawat Publication, New Delhi. 1994.

24. Hussain, Majid, *Resources Geography*, Anmol Publication Pvt. Ltd., New Delhi, 2000.

25. Jodhsingh, Maj., *War: Its Principles, Tactics and Strategies*, Surjeet Pub., Kamla Nagar, Delhi, 1980.

26. Johri, S. Maj., *Chinese Invasion of NEFA*, Himalayan Publisher, Luknow, 1968.

27. Kapoor, S.K., *International Law*, Central Law Agency, Allahabad, 1994.

28. Krishna Rao, K.V. Gen., *Prepare or Perish: A Study of National Security*, Lancer Publishers, New Delhi, 1991.

29. Kumar, Satish, *Year Book on Indias Foreign Policy 1985-1986*, Sage Pub., New Delhi, 1988.

30. Latkar, S.R. and A.S.Apte. *Political Geography*, Vidya Prakashan, Nagpur, 1998.

31. Louis, C. Peltier & G. Etzel Pearcy, *Military Geography*, East- West Press, Chennai, 1981.

32. Mishra, K.P., *Afghanistan in Crises*, Vikas Publication, Gaziabad (U.P.), 1981.

33. Muthib, *A Social & Economic Atlas of India*, Oxford Univ. Press, Delhi, 1987.

34. Mishra, R.N., *Indian Ocean and India's Security*, Mittal Publication, New Delhi, 1986.
35. Murthy, T.S. *Path of Peace: Studies on Sino-Indian Border Dispute*, ABC Publishing House, New Delhi, 1983.
36. Martin, Ira and Hami Blij, *Systematic Political Geography*, John Wiley and Sons, New York, 1973.
37. Modak, V.K., *The Para Military Forces: Need for Merger and Reorganisation, In Repowering National Security*, Aditya Prakashan, 1998, Mumbai.
38. Mishra, S.S., *Gulf War and Its Impact*, Radha Publication, New Delhi, 1993.
39. Nair, Balkrishnan, *Facts of Indian Defence*, S. Chand and Co. Ramnagar, New Delhi, 1985.
40. Norman, Pounds J., *Political Geography*, McGraw Hill Book Company, New York, 1972.
41. Philips, Bernard, *Illustrated Atlas of the World*, George Philip and Sons Ltd., London, 1980.
42. Pitre, K.G., Brig., *War History of Marathas, 1600-1848*, Books and Books Company, New Delhi, 1996.
43. Sukhwal, B.L., *Modern Political Geography of India*, Sterling Publication, Jalandhar, 1985.
44. Sukhwal, B.L., *A Political Geography*, Allied Publishers, Mumbai, 1971.
45. Sarin, Pramod, Brig. Retd., *Military Logistics: The Third Dimension*, Manas Publication, New Delhi, 2000.
46. Sali, M.L., *India China Border Dispute*, Ashish Publishing Corporation, New Delhi, 1998.
47. Sarkar, J.N., *Shivaji and His Times*, Orient Longman Publishers, New Delhi, 1966.
48. Sen, Surendranath, *Introduction to the Art of Warfare*, Sterling Publishers, New Delhi, 1979.
49. Sharma, R.C., *Growing Focus on Antarctica*, Rajesh Publication, New Delhi,1968.

50. Sharma, R.C. and Arya, D K, *Management Issues and Operational Planning for Indian Borders*, Scholar Publishing Forum, New Delhi. 1991.
51. Sharma, S.P., *India's Boundary and Territorial Dispute*, Vikas Publication, New Delhi, 1971.
52. Sharma, Satya, *Breaking the Ice in Antarctica: The First Indian Wintering in Antarctica*, New Age International Ltd., New Delhi, 2001.
53. Sing, Tejvir & Kaur Jagdish, *Studies In Economic Development: Himalaya Mountain & Men*, Print House, Lucknow, 1983
54. Singh, O.P., *The Himalaya: Nature, Man and Culture*, Rajesh Publication, New Delhi,1983.
55. Srivastava, L.N., *International Relations*, Surjeet Book Depot. New Delhi,1985
56. Srivastava, M.P., *Soviet Intervention in Afghanistan*, Ashoka Press, New Delhi.1980.
57. Venkateshwaran, A.L., *India's Defence Organisation*, Hindi Grantha Academy, Bhopal, 1973.
58. Winston S. Churchill, *The Second World War*, The Education Company Ltd. 1950, London (UK).

Articles and Seminar Papers

1. "Emergency Event Database Center for Research on Epidemiology of Disaster," EM-DAT, CRED University at Lauvain Belgium and *World Disaster Report, 2001.*
2. Adhikari, Shekhar, "H.J. Mackinder's Theory of Heartland: An Appraisal," *Indian Journal of Strategic Studies*, Vol. XXIII 2002, Defence Studies Department, University of Allahabad, Allahabad , (UP)
3. Ahlawat S. S. Capt., "The Siachin Impasse", *Indian Defense Review*, Lancer International, New Delhi, July 1988.
4. Apte. Mohan, "Year of National Disaster," *Lokrang*, Sunday, dated 25th Dec. 2005, Nasik.

5. Bedi, Kiran, "Civil Defence Mass Movement," *Lokmat*, 1st May 2006, Nasik, (M.S).
6. Bikash, B. Basu, "Role of Military Geography in Air Power," *USI Journal*, July-Sept-1991, Kashmir House, King George Avenue, New Delhi.
7. Chacko, Arun, "Siachen Glacier" *Indian Express*, Mumbai, 15th Nov. 1987.
8. Edward and Steven, "Latin America and Antarctica" *Current History* ,Vol. 82, Philadelphia, Nov/Feb-1983.
9. Godkar, Varsha Gajendra "Assurance for Security" *Sakal*, Nasik Edition, dated 21/04/1998.
10. Harvey, M.A. Maj., "Weather as a Factor in Tactical Planing", *Army Journal*, Vol. 5, No.56, 1991, The Russian Press Pvt. Ltd., Moscow.
11. Jadhav, V.Y., "War and Enviornment," *Maharashtra Geography: Science Journal*, Vol. XIII, No.2, July-Dec-1999, Marathi Version.
12. Jamuwal, N.S., "Management of Land Borders," *Strategic Analysis*, Vol. 26, No.3, July-Sept, 2002, IDSA Old JNU Campus, New Delhi, 67.
13. Jamuwal N.S., " Border Management: Dilemma of Guarding the India-Bangladesh Border," *Strategic Analysis*, Vol. 28, No. 1 Jan-March 2004, IDSA, Old JNU Campus, New Delhi 67.
14. Jathar, S., Maj.Gen., "Everything is for Oil" *Sakal*, Pune, dated 6th April 2003.
15. Khanna, O.P., "North East Region Security Challenges," *The Competition Master*, Vol. XXVIII, No.12, July-1968, Industrial Area, Chandigarh, India, 1987.
16. Khurana, G.S., "Cooperation among Security Forces: Imperatives for India and Southeast Asia", *Strategic Analysis*, Vol. 29, No. 2, April-June, 2005, I.D.S.A., New Delhi.
17. Khurana G.S., Maritime Security in the Indian Ocean: Convergence Plus Co-operation Equal Resonance, *Strategic Analysis*, Vol. 28, No-3, July-Sept. 2004, I.D.S.A., New Delhi.

18. Ladis, K.D. Kristof, "The Nature of Frontiers and Boundaries," Seminar paper, University of Chicago, USA, 1990.

19. Limaye, Raja Capt., "Environment as a Factor of Warfare," *Sakal*, Pune Edition, 26th April, 1998.

20. *Maharashtra Times*, Marathi Edition, Mumbai, 8th Oct 2001, Editorial Page.

21. Mathur, Anand, "Growing Influence of the Indian Ocean in Post Cold War Era & Its Implications for India," *Strategic Analysis*, Vol. 26, No. 4, Oct-Dec. 2002, I.D.S.A., New Delhi.

22. Narayan, Sunita, "First Pollutions and then Solutions Is It Affordable" *Sakal Weekly Journal*, Mumbai, 14th June 2006.

23. Pandarikonihan, N.V., Dir., "Water Resources Development: Present & Future," *Centre For Resources & Ocean Development*, Anna University, Madras, Oct. 1995.

24. Prasad, Rajendra "Sino Indian Border Dispute," Seminar Paper, Dept. of Defence. & Strategic Studies, University of Gorakhpur, Nov. 1984.

25. Raman, Maj. Gen., "Civil Defence for a Nuclear Age: Indian Context", *U.S.I. Journal*, April-June 1992.

26. Rodney, W. Jones, "U.S. Interest in the Indian Ocean Region," *Indian Journal of Defence Studies*, Univ. of Allhabad, 1983.(UP).

27. Sadhu, Arun "Why? For oil? *Maharashtra Times*, Mumbai, Marathi Edition, 22/11/2003

28. Singh, K.R., "Maritime Security: An Integrated Approach," *Seminar Paper*, School of International Studies, J.N.U., New Delhi, 1993.

29. Singh, R.S., Lt. Gen., "Infantry: Queen of Battle," *U.S.I. Journal*, New Delhi, April-June 1990.

30. Singh, R.S.N., "Engaging Inscrutable Myanmar," *Indian Defence Review*, Lancer Pub. New Delhi, 2004.

31. *The Times of India*, New Delhi, 29th Jan 1993.
32. Tripathi, V. & Pandey, S., "India's Maritime Security," *Prodeeding of XVIth National Congress for Defence Studies*, Department of Defence & Strategic Studies, University of Allahabad, 2005.(UP).
33. Varma, M.R.P., Maj., "Civil Defence In India: The Nature of Problem," *U.S.I. Journal*, July-Sept., Kashmir House, New Delhi, 1994.
34. Vohra, Sahadev, "Parameters of a Border Settlement with China," *Mainstream*, Vol. XXVIII, No. 23, New Delhi, March 31, 1990.
35. Vohra, Sahadev, "Sinkiang & Ladakh," *U.S.I. Journal*, New Delhi, Sept. 1990.

Encyclopedia, Web Sites & Others

1. "A New Survey of Universal Knowledge," *Encyclopaedia Britannica*, Vol. 10, INC, William Benton Pub., Chicago, 1959.
2. *The New Encyclopaedia Britannica Macropaedia, Chicago Encyclopaedia Britannica* Vol. 1, INC, 1974.
3. Precis on "Military Geography, Geopolitics, Strategic Minerals, Logistics Management, Grand Strategy, Strategy & Tactics", 1980-85, Prepared by Department of Defence & Strategic Studies, University of Pune, Pune 7.
4. http:/www.idsa.in/books.htm
5. www un.org/special-repl/
6. Ohrlls/11ds/default.htm land locked developing countries.
7. www.iwpr.net
8. www.google.search/
9. www.yahoo.search/
10. www.eurasia.net/

✣ ✣ ✣

INDEX